COOKING
WITH BEER

COOKING
WITH BEER

Over 65 recipes made with your favorite beers

mark dredge

DOG 'n' BONE

This edition published in 2021 by Dog 'n' Bone Books
An imprint of Ryland Peters & Small Ltd
20–21 Jockey's Fields   341 E 116th St
London WC1R 4BW   New York, NY 10029

www.rylandpeters.com

10 9 8 7 6 5 4 3 2 1

First published in 2016

A CIP catalog record for this book is available from the Library of
Congress and the British Library.

ISBN: 978 1 912983 46 9

Printed in China

Editor: Caroline West
Designer: Eoghan O'Brian
Photographer: Alex Luck (except page 131 by Peter Cassidy)
Stylist: Luis Peral
Home economist: Laura Urschel

Commissioning editor: Pete Jorgensen
Art director: Sally Powell
Production manager: Gordana Simakovic
Publishing manager: Penny Craig
Publisher: Cindy Richards

FSC
www.fsc.org
MIX
Paper from
responsible sources
FSC® C008047

USING THIS BOOK

I've tried to make these recipes as simple as possible. I'm
not a trained chef; I'm just a decent home cook and I'm
assuming you're the same—someone who likes good beers
and good food, and enjoys combining these in the kitchen.
If you're ever unclear on exact measurements or ingredients,
then here is a simple guide:

- If you see "1 bottle of beer" listed in the Ingredients, this
  means a regular-sized bottle—either the American 12fl oz
  (355ml) or the more worldly 11.2fl oz (330ml). The 25ml
  liquid difference between these won't make a difference
  to that recipe unless stated otherwise.

- I usually suggest a beer style to cook with and not an exact
  brand. Beers can vary greatly within their styles, so I've
  tried to give a tasting profile alongside the beer style (very
  aromatic Pale Ale with low bitterness, for example).

- All spoon measurements are level, unless stated otherwise.
  All eggs are US extra large (UK large) and ideally free-
  range. Milk is full fat or whole. Cream is heavy (double),
  unless stated.

- I always use sea salt crystals and never table salt in
  cooking. That's just a personal preference. If you're curing
  or brining, then always use sea salt or kosher salt.

- A recipe will often call for, say, "1–3 fresh chili peppers."
  This is because everyone has a different heat tolerance
  and preference. Simply make your own choice as to how
  much to add. Keeping the chili seeds is, of course, optional.

- The recipes give Imperial measurements (i.e. 2fl oz of beer,
  1 cup sugar, 375°F) and their metric equivalents (e.g. 60ml
  beer, 200g sugar, 190°C). I've done my best to ensure
  these conversions are as accurate as possible. Be sure not
  to mix your measurements, choose either the Imperial or
  metric and stick to it.

HOW TO STERILIZE A JAR

Recipes such as the Hoppy Peach Hot Sauce (page
40) and Weizen Ketchup (page 34) are stored in jars,
which will need sterilizing first. To sterilize a jar, wash
the glass and lid in hot, soapy water and place upside-
down in a 250°F/120°C/Gas ½ oven to dry for around
30 minutes, then remove. If you are using a Kilner jar
with a rubber neck, remove this and don't put it in the
oven. Where appropriate, fill the jars when still warm.

A BASIC BEER BRINE

I use a brine in many recipes and there's a simple and
consistent base brine for all of these: in a sealable
container, combine a bottle of beer, the equivalent amount of water
(typically enough to cover whatever you're brining–if in
doubt use less water than beer), 3 tablespoons of salt,
3 tablespoons of sugar, plus additional flavors (e.g. spices,
citrus, herbs). Leave for 8–24 hours.

CONTENTS

INTRODUCTION

I was standing around a scummy hob in my university house the first time I added beer to something I was cooking. I was drinking a bottle of lager while making a risotto; I didn't have any wine, so I just used beer instead. It tasted good.

I had no idea that those few splashes of cheap lager would lead to this book a decade later. Back then I was just cooking with what was literally to hand and adapting a recipe by using a different ingredient (which also happened to be an ingredient I preferred to wine). In the ten years since I left university, I've cooked with every kind of beer there is, using it in more ways than I can remember, with some of the dishes tasting great and some tasting incredible. The best thing about this approach to cooking is being able to take a beer I love and transform it into something delicious to eat. There's a wonderful alchemy in that.

Today, cooking with beer is growing in popularity around the world, assisted by our increasing knowledge of beer and food and a general culinary curiosity that naturally prompts us to use the huge variety of beers now available in the kitchen. Countless bars and brewpubs use beer in different dishes; Michelin-starred restaurants cook with beer; and there are restaurants specializing in beer-infused food. There are also websites and YouTube channels dedicated to beer cooking, and it's going way beyond old classics, such as pies and stews, and creating a new evolution of what beer cuisine is and what it can be. And that's exciting.

However, we can't look too far forward before having a look backward, and checking out those classic dishes that have been cooked for generations, where the traditional drinking nations all have a few dishes that use beer. The Belgian cuisine à la bière is the most prolific in terms of cooking with beer, incorporating it in a range of recipes, including soups, sauces, pâtés, mussels, carbonnade, and puddings—these also use all their many types of beer, from sour cherry beers to lively golden ales to dark, strong monastery brews. In Britain and Ireland, there's pies, stews, chutneys, cakes, and batter for the famous fried fish. In Germany and Czech Republic, there's sausages in beer and braises, plus sauces to go with hunks of meat. And these are just the few recipes still around today. If we look back a century or two, or even five or six, it'd be very

different because beer was undoubtedly more prevalent in cooking then. In the past, beer was predominantly homebrewed, so it was in the kitchen next to the food—in many ways it was a food in its own right, something with nutritional and caloric value, as well as an ingredient that contributed flavor at a time when people didn't have stacked spice racks or the kinds of sauces and condiments we routinely reach for today.

"There's not a huge amount of historical stuff, but that, I suspect, is because cooking with ale/beer was so natural that nobody bothered to record it," says beer historian Martyn Cornell. The few older recipes are interesting: stews that were authentic Neolithic-style dishes; 12th-century recipes for stewing fish in ale; recipes using up soured beer in place of vinegars and in pickling liquids. In *Beer and Vittels* Elizabeth Craig writes: "In Georgian and Victorian days beer was freely used in the kitchen." There are also many old Belgian books dedicated to the topic. But, in a way, none of this really matters now because newer brewers and chefs aren't looking at old braises. Instead, they're looking at contemporary cooking, they're using current food influences, and they're developing them with beer.

We have limitless options and possibilities when cooking with beer, whether it's a simple stir fry or an impressive dessert. What makes it particularly interesting is the huge range of beer types available and the flavors and qualities they can give a dish—a smoked Porter that tastes like bonfired bacon; treacly Imperial Stouts; raisin and port-like Quadrupels; IPAs with incredible tropical fruit and citrus aromas; sour beers like a squeeze of lemon juice. We can then decide how to use those beers and work out what they might give to a recipe: the smoky Porter makes an amazing pizza dough and gives a savory depth in a brine for chicken; Quadrupel makes an incredible ice cream, but can also add sweetness to bread; and the IPA can transform a chocolate mousse with citrusy bitterness, but also add malt complexity to a mac 'n' cheese. No other liquid family can offer so much in the kitchen.

I love cooking with beer because it has such enormous breadth, depth, and versatility as an ingredient, working in so many different ways and in so many different recipes. I love how you can add your favorite beer to a dish or adapt favorite recipes by including a beer—now who wouldn't be interested in doing that? This book features some of my favorite methods for cooking with beer; I've generally overlooked the classics and sought to find new ways of using beer in the kitchen.

USING BEER IN THE KITCHEN

Beer is one of the simplest ingredients to cook with. If a recipe includes a liquid–water, wine, stock, or milk–then you can use beer instead. You can use beer for baking, brining, and braising. You can put it in a quick pasta sauce or a slow stew, or use it in a dressing or cake frosting. Beer is also an incredibly versatile liquid, with a huge range of flavors and tastes, meaning it can contribute a bready sweetness, chocolatey richness, tropical-fruit freshness, or lemony acidity, and so much more.

Although effective and versatile, beer is also a challenging ingredient to cook with. It's essentially flavored and fermented water–over 90 percent of what's in your beer glass is water. The grain used in the brewing process leaves color, richness, and some flavor. The hops are beer's aromatic seasonings and can be earthy, floral, citrusy, herbal, tropical, and more, but they are also bitter, which is often a negative in the kitchen. The alcohol is hidden from sight but brought out by cooking, which is a good thing, as it gives the food greater depth and complex fullness of flavor. The yeast in beer can give a range of qualities, from peppery and fruity through to sour, but that often doesn't influence the food. While beer might be a drink that's full of flavor, trying to get those flavors into your food requires some skill.

Cooking with beer doesn't always turn out as you might expect. For example, imagine an IPA that smells like grapefruit and mango. It'd be amazing to capture that aroma as a flavor, but it doesn't work like that because the aroma is the first thing to go when you cook with it. Lager, despite its relative simplicity, can give a really good depth to a dish, that hard-to-define alcohol quality that enriches food. You might think that reducing the beer in a pan might intensify all the flavors into a thick beer syrup, but that rarely happens and, instead, you boil away all the nice aromas and kick out the bitterness (dark, strong Belgian beers are a nice exception to this, though you still need to add sugar). The truth is that you never quite know what qualities will pull through when cooking with a beer, but there are tricks and tips on page 15 to help you out.

This book is all about cooking with beer. If you think that's a wasteful use of a delicious drink, then you're probably missing the point of what this book is setting out to achieve. In many cases, you can use an affordable bottle of beer that costs the same as a chicken breast or bag of carrots–you don't have to cook with rare or expensive beers (although, of course, you can use them if you wish). Often the recipes only call for a small amount of liquid, leaving the rest for you to drink, which is always fantastic because you really can't beat cooking a delicious meal with a beer in your hand.

PAIRING BEER AND FOOD

Most of the recipes in this book come with suggestions for beers to drink with the dish. This is my approach to beer and food pairing. (For more on this, check out my book *Beer and Food*, which goes into more detail.)

BRIDGE

Think about forming a bridge between the beer and the food by connecting similar flavors or qualities. For example, try Belgian Witbier, which is infused with coriander seed and citrus, with a Southeast Asian curry; the aniseed and fragrant spicy flavors of a Belgian Dubbel with a Moroccan lamb tagine; a Porter with a chargrilled steak; smoked trout with a Rauchbier; or Pale Ale's citrus and resinous flavors with a garlic, lemon, and herb chicken. The bridge of flavors naturally draws these elements together and helps them to enhance each other.

BALANCE

There are times when food can be powerful in both flavor and texture, and adding an equally dominant beer to the dish can overpower everything. In this case, aim to balance the flavors or highlight different qualities or ingredients in subtle ways. You're most likely to do this when the food has an extremity of flavor—often fat, salt, or chili heat. Hefeweizen with spicy Thai fishcakes; refreshing Pale Lager with an Indian curry; Sweet Stout with jerk chicken; Pale Ale with a cheeseburger; sour beer with smoked mackerel. The food can also work to balance bitterness in a beer: fries or potato chips with IPA or strong cheese with Double IPA.

BOOST

Sometimes you'll combine beer with food and they work together in an unexpected way, boosting the qualities and thus your enjoyment of both—typically, you'll get more qualities out of drink and dinner than before. A sour cherry beer brings out the fruitier flavors in dark chocolate (that's the classic go-to boost pairing); carrot cake and Double IPA are amazing together; a boozy, raisiny Barley Wine is like a sweet chutney with blue cheese; smoke and citrus set each other off, whether it's barbecued meat with Pale Ale or Rauchbier with grilled salmon and lemon; while sometimes it's a condiment which can help the combo, with the best example being steak and horseradish with Oatmeal Stout, where together the beer and sauce enhance the meat's flavor.

LOCAL

Look at local food and the most popular beer styles produced in the region and you'll find they typically work together naturally. British Bitter with the Cheddar cheese in a ploughman's lunch; Californian-brewed Pale Ale with fish tacos; Munich Helles with a fresh pretzel; Italian Pilsner with pizza; Japanese Rice Lager with yakitori; or Trappist Ales paired with the monastery's cheeses.

INTENSITY AND TEXTURE

This is an important consideration because you want to match the intensity of a dish with the intensity of a beer (think Pilsner versus Belgian Tripel), while also thinking about the textures that each brings (think lively carbonation versus smooth, full-bodied beers). You wouldn't open a fragrant, effervescent Saison to go with gooey chocolate brownies because the beer would taste horrible with the rich sweetness of the cake. And you wouldn't put a plate of delicate charcuterie with a glass of thick, strong Imperial Stout because it'd be like pouring chocolate syrup over the meat. But put the delicate Saison with the cured meat and they share a similar subtle, spicy depth, just as the brownie and Stout are both chewy and chocolatey.

THE FIVE TASTES

The five tastes interact with each other in interesting ways, so it helps to understand how they work when combining beer and food. Umami is a rich savory taste (think soy sauce, cured meat, aged cheese). I think beer has an inherently umami edge as a result of the malting process, plus certain characteristics of the yeast. This is very important because umami naturally enhances the flavor of food and gives it more depth, meaning that beer can also act as a flavor booster. Bitter beer can be softened by salty and fatty foods. Sweet beer likes either very savory foods or needs to be drunk with an equally sweet food. Sourness is refreshing and quenching, and works well with salt and fatty richness. Salt is great with beer because the drink is refreshing against it.

CHILI HEAT

Chili heat is an irritation that gives a burning sensation. A highly carbonated beer will aggravate that irritation. Similarly, bitterness will poke at the burn and make it unpleasant, so try to drink smoother, sweeter, and softer beers with spicy food. Adding a cooling ingredient, such as yogurt or avocado, or fragrant herbs like mint, to the dish can also help. Also consider mustard, horseradish, wasabi, pepper, and ginger, because they are pungent and powerful like chili.

A GUIDE TO BEER STYLES

PALE LAGER

The most dominate beer type in the world, the Pale Lager category is broader than most drinkers realize. It starts at the bottom with bland mass-market brews and can reach all the way to complex and extraordinary beers. German Helles and Czech Pilsners are the classics; Helles tends to be softer, rounder, and less bitter than the drier, snappier Pilsners. Modern versions can use hops to give more aroma and bitterness—these tend to be better for drinking than cooking, as the delicate aromas are lost in the cooking process.

DRINK WITH: Classic Central European beer food like pretzels and grilled meats. Also great with spicy food and Asian curries, plus salads and picnic foods such as quiches or simple sandwiches.

IN THE KITCHEN: Great for beer brines. You can also use it to bake delicate doughs (especially pretzels and pizza), or turn a can of lager into a curry feast (see Leftover Lager Curry, on page 94). The better lagers give more complexity and depth, especially when slow-cooked in a stew or goulash, but you can equally add a can of crap lager to turn the dish into something delicious, which is a brilliant use of beer that you don't want to drink.

DARK LAGER

Until the middle of the 19th century, all lagers would've been dark. Today these remain a traditional beer type in Central Europe. The roasted grains that turn these beers dark give a toasty, roasty, and nutty depth to the drink, making it a great beer to go with food as it shares the subtle qualities of caramelized and cooked food (think grilled steak and fresh toast). Dunkels tend to be more subtle in the dark malts, as if you've got a Helles dusted with cocoa and toast, while Schwarzbier is darker, drier, and roastier.

DRINK WITH: Asian noodles are excellent, German and Czech stews like goulash work well, steak and roasted meat are great. Middle Eastern salads and grilled meat (think kofte) are also good.

IN THE KITCHEN: Dark lagers are really good to cook with. They work well in Asian dishes, in slow-braised meat dishes (classic Central-European-style), and in brines for steak or pork, as they'll add a depth of meatiness. Try in tomato-based pasta sauces for extra oomph (for example, see Beer Meatballs and Tomato Sauce with Spaghetti, on page 78).

WHEAT BEER

There are two main types of Wheat Beer: Belgian and German. Belgian Witbier is typically brewed using coriander seed and orange peel, and has a peppery, spicy finish; German Hefeweizen is a bit sweeter and rounder, giving banana and bubble gum aromas with some peppery, clove-like depth. You might see American versions too, which tend to be smooth, yet dry, and without much yeast aroma but often plenty of hops. They all share a relatively full body and smooth texture, are low in bitterness, and high in yeast-produced aromas. The German style extends out to include Dunkelweizen, a dark wheat beer, and Weizenbock, a strong Hefeweizen.

DRINK WITH: Good with spicy foods, having the ability to balance heat by wrapping spice in smoothness, where Southeast Asian is especially good with all types; Witbier is best with more aromatic dishes, Hefeweizen with creamier dishes. Mexican is also a good match.

IN THE KITCHEN: Definitely good in the kitchen. I frequently bake with Hefeweizen, so try this in pretzels (see Soft Beer Pretzel Bites with Beer Mustard, on page 118), doughs, and cakes. The low bitterness means it works well in Asian food or to give an interesting flavor to brines. Witbier is very nice in Southeast Asian curries or fish cakes.

SAISON

Saisons can differ greatly, though we usually expect a dry beer with a firm and substantial, but not sweet, body, plus some yeast-derived aromas such as banana, lemon peel, or peppery funk. Some might be sub 4.0% ABV, while others will be over 6.0% ABV. They might be sour or bitter, while newer versions getting lots of late-hop additions are very fruity and aromatic. Bière de Garde, a member of the extended Farmhouse Beer family, is similar to Saison, but sweeter, stronger, and fuller-bodied.

DRINK WITH: Saisons are top food beers, particularly classics such as Saison Dupont. Southeast Asian cuisine is as excellent with Saison as farmhouse cheeses and cured meat, while both steak and lobster also work well. You can pretty much eat everything with Saison and it'll be a decent match.

IN THE KITCHEN: Although better with food, rather than in it, I like to use Saison in curries (see Saison-Spiked Fish Laksa, on page 92) and fish cakes, where it gives a boost to lemon grass, ginger, and pepper flavors. Bière de Garde works in the classic coq à la bière—or chicken stewed in beer.

BELGIAN BLONDE, GOLDEN ALE, AND TRIPEL

These are together because they are all pale in color, of Belgian origin or inspiration, and share similar flavors: light, toasty malt, a dry finish, and some peppery yeast. Blondes are the lightest in alcohol and range from very bitter to sticky and sweet (in a bad way). As you step that up, you get to Golden Ale and Tripel (think Duvel and Westmalle Tripel for classics), boozy, bold, yet gloriously elegant and refreshing, with a spicy dryness at the end.

DRINK WITH: Versatile and food-friendly, their fizz is refreshing, while the base of the beer is strong enough to handle big flavors. Fried food is good, as are creamy curries; roast pork or chicken is excellent; all are good with sausages, cured meat, or strong cheese.

IN THE KITCHEN: The alcohol strength of these beers lends a wine-like flavor to slow-cooking. I also like to use them as you would a seasoning or squeeze of lemon, pouring over a splash or two near the end of the cooking process for curries or creamy pasta sauces (see Duvel and Anchovy Sauce for Pasta, on page 83). Blondes are brilliant in cheese sauce (see Ultimate Beer Cheese Sauce, on page 104).

BELGIAN BROWN, DUBBEL, AND QUADRUPEL

From bready Browns to teacake Dubbels to Christmas cake Quads, these beers vary greatly, though sit together here (like Blondes to Tripels) because of their color and origin. Browns aren't as common, but are toasty and easy to drink. Dubbels tend toward raisins and brown bread with a dusting of spice, while Quads step that up to be bigger and boozier, rummy and plummy, and deeply interesting; these are the traditional beers brewed in Trappist monasteries.

DRINK WITH: Browns and Dubbels are great food beers, especially with grilled red meat, Belgian stews such as carbonnade, and smoked or barbecued food, as well as a surprisingly good general match for Chinese and North African food. Quadrupels work better with desserts such as cheesecake, chocolate mousse, or fruitcake, plus it's like chutney on the side of a cheeseboard.

IN THE KITCHEN: Use these to make the classic carbonnade and other stews. They also work brilliantly on barbecued and grilled meats, either as a brine or in a sauce, giving a spicy sweetness. They add great flavor to cakes and doughs, and are strong enough to flavor cream for a panna cotta (see Dubbel Panna Cotta, on page 140).

SOUR BEER AND FRUIT BEER

This could be a classic Gueuze, a beer aged in barrels for years that blends old and young liquids to create an acidic, lemony, funky, complex drink like a sharp Champagne. It could be a Red or Bruin, sweet-sour beers that have an acetic edge like good balsamic vinegar. Or it could be a modern "fast sour," turned tart with bacteria (and often brewed with fruit). These all tend to be low in alcohol and the acidity should be quenching and not challenging (though it's often negatively sour). Fruit beers can be sour, though they often have an acidic edge. In general, I don't like artificially sweet fruit beers, but they can be decent drunk with food and when cooking.

DRINK WITH: Think of the best ones like Champagne. It's a refreshing, enlivening drink that has a tartness that increases the appetite and has the ability to cut through rich flavors like a squeeze of lemon. Fried foods, pâtés, creamy or funky cheeses, and cured meat are all good. Fruited fast sours can be excellent with Mexican food—think of them like the lime on a taco. The sweet-sourness in a cherry beer can be unbeatable with chocolate.

IN THE KITCHEN: You can use these beers like a vinegar or citrus juice. They make great pickles, excellent salad dressings, and a good seasoning for Asian or Mexican food. If you slow-cook with them, they give depth, not acidity. Bakes (especially sweet ones) and brines also work well. You can even use sour beer to cure fish like a classic ceviche (see Sour Beer Ceviche, on page 48).

GOLDEN ALE AND BEST BITTER

Golden Ale, as we know it today, arrived in the 1980s as an English antidote to the unstoppable rise of European lagers. Bright gold, with gentle English malts that give a toasty depth, then floral, fragrant hops for balance and not bold bitterness. Years later, they still have the same base, only the hop levels have increased and the aromas have been loaded with more citrusy American hops. Best Bitters range from pale gold (where you'd also call them English Pales Ales) to deep brown. Their key qualities are "sessionability"—that rare kind of beer that's still appealing after four pints—and balance, which tends toward bitterness. Earthy and woody English hops are at their core.

DRINK WITH: Golden Ales are summery, and work with outdoor pub-garden food such as barbecues, salads, grilled fish, roasted vegetables, quiches, hot dogs, and burgers. Best Bitters are for indoor pub-grub like fish and chips, good cheese, Scotch eggs, and sausage rolls.

IN THE KITCHEN: It is unusual to cook with these beers. The gentle malt flavor, plus the relatively high bitterness, means they don't offer much in the kitchen. The best uses are in brines for grilled meat or you can use the Best Bitter in a pie or stew—just balance it with something sweet such as onions or root vegetables.

PALE ALE

By Pale Ale we mean American Pale Ale as that's become the standard for the style. It's going to be a beer that's between blonde and amber, between 4.0–6.0% ABV, and dominated by the aroma and flavor of American hops to give citrus, pine resin, floral, and tropical fruit. The malt might be subtle or sweet and the bitterness could be balanced or aggressive. These are some of the most popular beers in the world and most craft breweries make one.

DRINK WITH: These beers stand up to big dishes like barbecues and smoked food—the smoke flavor is especially good with citrusy hops. Also decent with Mexican food, burgers, and sandwiches, fried chicken, mac 'n' cheese. Basically everything that we consider to be "American food."

IN THE KITCHEN: The hops make Pale Ale hard to use in the kitchen, as you tend to lose the aroma first and then the bitterness barges in. Try using in brines for pork or chicken wings (see Beer Hot Wings, on page 40) or combine with rich or sweet ingredients such as cheeses or cakes.

AMERICAN IPA

The most popular craft beer style in the world today, IPA is all about the flavor, bitterness, and aroma of hops. A powerful beer, it's often strong in alcohol, with a subtly sweet malt depth, which is there to balance all the hops and their bitterness. The hops give it the classic aroma of citrus juice and pith, tangy pine, and tropical fruit. The style is constantly evolving and different everywhere you go, though the current trend is toward very pale beers with huge juicy tropical-fruit aromas and a relatively low bitterness.

DRINK WITH: It's similar to Pale Ale, so goes with similar foods. Try to avoid too much spice, though, because hops and chili heat can get angry. Instead, you want richness and fat to go up against the hops, so a loaded cheeseburger, fries, ribs, brisket, strong Cheddar cheese, bar snacks, and even desserts like carrot or apple cake are good.

IN THE KITCHEN: The hops make it challenging to include IPA in recipes (it can taste like perfume in your dinner). The trick is to put it in strong foods that have a lot of richness, such as the IPA and Cheddar Cheese Barley Risotto (see page 91) and some citrus-based desserts.

THE EXTENDED IPA FAMILY

IPA is now so much more than just one type of beer. Today, IPA really means that you're going to get a beer that's very hoppy—both in bitterness and aroma. It then requires a prefix to tell us exactly what we might get and there are many variations. White, Red, Brown, and Black reveal the color (White is like a hoppy wheat beer); Imperial or Double are stronger versions, while Session is a low-ABV take on IPA. If you see English, German, Czech, Australian, or New Zealand IPAs, then they contain hops from those countries. With food, the best advice is to imagine the flavors in the beer and how they might naturally work with a dish: for example, a Black IPA is brilliant with smoked brisket, a Session IPA is great with dishes such as fish tacos, and a New Zealand IPA, with its tropical fruit and lime, works well with Thai-influenced dishes.

PORTER AND STOUT

There isn't a huge difference between Stout and Porter today, with the two types of beer overlapping, though I wouldn't be surprised if they soon start pulling away from one another, with Porter becoming a little lighter and nuttier and Stout darker, drier, and dominated by roasted malts. In general, though, you can expect dark brown to black beers, with the malts giving toast, dark chocolate, coffee, and roasted nuts. Most will be bitter, but not aromatically hopped. They can be refreshing or satisfying, while "nitro" versions will be very full-bodied and smooth. If you see Oatmeal Stout or Milk Stout, then these are creamier, smoother, lusher styles, typically fuller-bodied and sweeter.

DRINK WITH: The richer versions are ideal for hearty dishes like pies and stews, while lighter versions are great matches for tomato-based pasta sauces, grilled meat, offal, oily fish, and spicy grilled lamb or pork chops. Oatmeal and Milk versions are some of the best food beers you'll find, being great with Japanese noodles, fried rice, and teriyaki. They're brilliant at balancing heat, so try with coconut-based Indian curries, jerk chicken, and Cajun food. Stronger versions are good with oatmeal cookies, chocolate brownies, or maple syrup pancakes.

IN THE KITCHEN: These are great cooking beers. The classic is beef and Stout stew, long-braised with onions and root vegetables, and served with mashed potato. Another classic is Welsh Rarebit. They're excellent in a cheese sauce; in a Bolognese or meatball sauce (see Beer Bolognese, on page 79, and Beer Meatballs and Tomato Sauce with Spaghetti, on page 78); when slow-cooking ribs in beer; or for making condiments like barbecue sauce or ketchup. Oatmeal and Milk versions are great in noodles, used alongside soy sauce; perfect in pulled pork or a batch of beer chili (see Beer Chili Buns, on page 44); plus cookies and chocolate desserts (see Stout Chocolate Banana Pudding, on page 124).

IMPERIAL PORTER AND STOUT

The Imperial (or Double) prefix on any beer style tells you it will be a bigger version of that beer. With Imperial Porter and Stout—which includes Oatmeal and Milk versions, any of which may also contain edible ingredients like vanilla, chocolate, or coffee—that means big dark beers, normally 9.0% ABV and above, thick and rich, smooth and intense, with dark chocolate and coffee dominating the flavors before a boozy finish. You might also find barrel-aged versions, which are often left in Bourbon barrels for a few months, where the base beer sucks vanilla and toffee qualities from the wood.

DRINK WITH: This is a dessert beer, so drink it with chocolate puddings, roasted bananas, pancakes with maple syrup, crème brûlée, and ice cream. Think about it this way: if you could pour chocolate sauce on the side of a dessert, then it'll work with Imperial Porter and Stout. A good blue cheese is a great alternative. Lighter and less-intense versions can be superb with barbecued meats.

IN THE KITCHEN: It's good cooking beer. Try dark chocolate cakes and mousses or beer ice cream, or go savory with an Imperial Stout slow-cooked chili, braised ribs (see Boilermaker Ribs, on page 60), brisket, or baked beans—it might be an expensive addition, but it leaves a flavor and depth that's hard to find in other ingredients, giving sweetness, umami roast, chocolate, and the complexity of alcohol.

SMOKED BEER

This is a fairly niche category of beers, of which not a huge amount are made, but they get space here because they are excellent with food. During the malting process, the barley is put over a wood fire where it sucks up all the smoky flavors, which are then blown into the beer. Rauchbier is the classic German version and it's like a glass of liquid smoked sausage that's actually refreshingly interesting to drink. Others might be a smoked version of another style, often Stout or Porter, with the smoke flavor ranging from bonfire to barbecue to bacon.

DRINK WITH: The beery smoke makes meat taste meatier—bacon is excellent, sausages are great, as is roast chicken or just a really good steak or pork chop. They work almost universally well because the smoke is like an injection of tasty umami—try pizza, yakitori, or ramen, roasted pumpkin or squash, Mexican food, grilled mushrooms, spaghetti Bolognese, and so much more.

IN THE KITCHEN: My first expectation when cooking with Rauchbier was that it'd make the food taste as if it had been in a smoker for hours. But, as the smoke aroma is volatile, it is extinguished by cooking. You still get a hint of savory smoke in stewed or slow-cooked dishes, though you get more of the toasty, sweet malt depth. You can use it in tomato sauces for pizza or pasta; in doughs for pizza or flatbreads; in a sauce to go with steak; in brines for chicken or pork; and even to cure your own bacon (see Beer-cured Bacon Sandwich, on page 20). It's a great cooking beer.

TOP TIPS FOR COOKING WITH BEER

- **CHOOSE THE RIGHT BEER** Certain beer styles are especially good in the kitchen, so aim to cook with Dark Lager, Belgian Dubbel and Quadrupel, Sweet Stouts, and Hefeweizen. These are mostly low in bitterness, but have a great malt or yeast depth.

- **MATCH BEER AND FOOD FLAVORS** Think about what the beer tastes like and use similar-tasting ingredients to enhance these flavors—try using cinnamon and dried fruit with a Dubbel; lemon and pepper in something cooked with Tripel; caramelized onions to match sweet malt flavors, whether in an IPA or dark ale; fennel and ground coriander to pick out the yeast in Saison and Witbier; Imperial Stout with dark chocolate; Dark Lager or Stout have a similar malty, savory taste to soy sauce; or browning the outside of good-quality meat before adding Porter.

- **SLOW-COOK WITH BEER** This cooking method is excellent because the bitterness will eventually integrate or disappear (who knows how, why, or where it goes, but it does). While the dish bubbles away, the water evaporates, leaving behind the richness of alcohol and malt. You are essentially cooking out the water and bringing forward the inner beer flavor. However, this method doesn't necessarily retain many of the beer's subtler qualities. To solve this, reserve a small amount of the beer and then add this to the dish before serving to perk up the beer flavor.

- **BRINE WITH BEER** This is one of the best ways to use beer in the kitchen. You simply mix beer, sugar, and salt, plus whatever else you like. Put meat in that brine for a day and it'll take on loads of flavor, while remaining wonderfully moist. You can also pick ingredients to enhance the beer flavor (for example, Pale Ale with orange peel and garlic or Witbier with coriander seeds).

- **ENHANCE MALT SWEETNESS** Most of the recipes in this book, even the savory ones, include something sweet (such as sugar, honey, or maple syrup). Malt has a sweet flavor, so adding sweetness will enhance that. More importantly, malt has the ability to balance bitterness.

- **REDUCE HOP BITTERNESS** This is an unavoidable issue and no one really wants to eat bitter food. Sweet ingredients such as caramelized onions, root vegetables, cooked meat, or simply some sugar will all help. Never boil a hoppy beer quickly. Always avoid adding beer directly to a hot pan—use a little stock or water first and then add the beer. Basically, try to avoid using very bitter beers unless it's in rich and sweet recipes (such as the Double IPA Carrot Cake, on page 122, or the Chocolate Orange Double IPA Mousse, on page 138).

- **USE BEER AS SEASONING** Beer aromas are volatile and applying heat to them generally makes them disappear. Not cooking the beer is one way to avoid this. This could mean using the beer as a seasoning, as you would a squeeze of citrus juice, or putting it in a salad dressing or a cake's frosting.

- **POUR THE BEER FIRST** You rarely want the carbonation in a beer when cooking and you'll typically need to use the beer at room temperature (although this won't make too much difference unless specifically stated in the recipe). You could pour the beer a few hours before cooking or just pour it in a cup and stir with a spoon for a minute or two.

- **SOUR OR NOT?** If you cook sour beer, you won't get a sour-tasting dish, but if you add it uncooked, then it will leave behind its acidity.

- **BALANCE LIQUIDS** Beer can typically replace any liquid in a recipe, whether stock, milk, water, or a different alcohol. You may want to use only beer or just replace some of the liquid with a smaller amount of beer. I usually start by going half-and-half with beer and the other liquid, then see how it works, and make adjustments (if needed) the next time. Also, just because Stout has a roasted richness that's similar to soy sauce doesn't mean you can leave out the soy—you'll still need both, with the beer bringing an additional flavor element.

- **TAKE A SUBTLE APPROACH** You don't always want a dish to taste strongly of beer. Instead, think of the beer as just one of many ingredients in a recipe, something that adds its own quality but doesn't dominate. Take salt as another example: yes, it's sometimes important in a dish, but too much can ruin the food. If you use beer, it will add its own qualities, whether you put in two ounces or two bottles of it.

- **DRINK THE BEER TOO** The beer you've cooked with will often taste great served with the food, so get an extra bottle and see what qualities remain from the cooking process.

- **SAVE SOME BEER** If you're planning to cook with a beer, drink most of it but leave some in the bottle. Just put plastic wrap (clingfilm) over the bottle and keep in the refrigerator until needed in the kitchen.

- **KEEP IT SIMPLE AND FUN** Perhaps the most important tip of all: just enjoy cooking with beer. It doesn't have to be difficult or fancy, but really it should always be fun.

CHAPTER 1

BREAKFAST

COFFEE STOUT PANCAKES

This is a brilliant, boozy brunch recipe: the kind you can mix up and cook quickly, before taking it back to eat in bed. Use the strongest Stout you have, ideally one that's brewed with coffee, where a shot of espresso boosts the roasted richness. I like to serve it with some sliced banana on top.

MAKES 6-8

1¾ cup (225g) all-purpose (plain) flour
1 teaspoon baking powder
½ teaspoon salt
½ teaspoon ground cinnamon
3 tablespoons sugar
1 egg, beaten
2 tablespoons natural yogurt
⅔ cup (150ml) milk
⅓ cup (100ml) Imperial Stout
1 shot espresso (optional, but good)
1 punnet blueberries
Butter or vegetable oil, for frying
  (I like to use coconut oil)
Maple syrup, to serve

1 Combine all the dry ingredients (apart from the blueberries) in a bowl and all the wet ingredients (except the maple syrup) in a second bowl. Combine the dry and liquid ingredients, mixing well until you have a thick pancake batter.

2 Add as many blueberries as you wish—a small handful per pancake is about right.

3 Heat a small amount of butter or cooking oil in a large frying pan before pouring in some pancake batter. Cook the pancake for a few minutes before flipping it over and cooking it on the other side for two more minutes.

4 Once cooked, eat the pancakes straightaway, drizzled with maple syrup and a few extra berries, or stack them up and keep in a warm oven until needed.

EAT IT WITH...

The rest of the Stout you cooked with. Or open another bottle of Coffee Stout. You might as well treat yourself to something good if you're drinking beer with breakfast so look for Mikkeller Beer Geek Brunch Weasel, BrewDog Cocoa Psycho or Founder's Breakfast Stout.

BEER-CURED BACON SANDWICH
AND SMOKY BACON KETCHUP

SERVES 8

FOR CURING THE BACON

2¼lb (1kg) pork belly, skin removed
2 bottles of Smoked Beer
2 cups (500ml) water
3oz (85g) sea salt
Heaping ½ cup (130g) brown sugar
¼ cup (50ml) maple syrup
1 tablespoon black peppercorns

FOR THE SMOKY BACON KETCHUP
MAKES 2-3 X 15FL OZ (450ML) JARS

Olive oil, for cooking
18oz (500g) fresh tomatoes, roughly diced
5 garlic cloves (preferably smoked garlic)
1 tablespoon smoked paprika
1 large red onion, finely chopped
3½oz (100g) smoked bacon, finely chopped
14oz (400g) can plum tomatoes
1 teaspoon each smoked paprika, cayenne pepper, and five spice
¾ cup (150g) brown sugar or maple syrup
¾ cup (200ml) Smoked Beer or Porter
⅓ cup (100ml) malt vinegar
Salt and black pepper

TO SERVE: Sandwich the bacon in some thick fresh bread with some beer ketchup.

Yes, this is beer-cured bacon you can make at home. And you can also serve it with Smoky Bacon Ketchup. You could even add some cooked pieces of bacon to the Beer Soda Bread recipe on page 116 and turn this into the ultimate beer-bacon feast. The bacon might take around a week to cure, but the preparation time is less than it takes to drink a pint.

TO MAKE THE BEER-CURED BACON

1 To cure the bacon, place all the ingredients, apart from the pork, in a large, deep container (the pork needs lots of room, so ensure the container is large enough).

2 Stir to combine the ingredients, then place the pork in the container. Place a plate or small chopping board on top of the pork to keep it submerged. Cover the container and keep the pork in the refrigerator for 5–7 days.

3 Take the container out of the fridge. Drain the liquid and dry the pork with paper towels. Return to the fridge uncovered for 24 hours.

4 Simply slice the pork and cook it as you would regular bacon (you'll probably get thick slices that are more like bacon chops unless you have extraordinary knife skills).

TO MAKE THE BEER KETCHUP

1 The ketchup can be made months in advance or you can cook it fresh. To begin, preheat the oven to 400°F/200°C/Gas 6. Place a tablespoon of olive oil in a baking dish and roast the tomatoes with three garlic cloves and the smoked paprika for 20 minutes.

2 Meanwhile, gently soften the onion in a tablespoon of olive oil in a large pan. Chop the remaining 2 garlic cloves and add them to the onion, stirring for a minute. Add the bacon to the pan and cook for a further 2–3 minutes.

3 Add the roasted tomatoes, then pour in the canned tomatoes, followed by the remaining ingredients. Season with salt and black pepper, according to taste. Simmer for 30 minutes with the lid on and then a further 30 minutes with the lid off (you can increase this time by up to 60 minutes if you want a thicker, richer sauce).

4 Allow the sauce to cool before blending into a smooth ketchup. Pour into sterilized jars (see page 4 for guidance on sterilizing).

EAT IT WITH...

Oatmeal Stout just works for breakfast. It's lulling in its smooth sweetness and has the roasted qualities of coffee, where the sweetness in the bacon is made to taste richer by the beer. Try Good People's Coffee Oatmeal Stout in the US, Nail Stout in Australia, or the classic Sam Smith Oatmeal Stout.

WEISSBIER FRITTATA

SERVES 2

6 eggs

3 tablespoons Hefeweizen

1 tablespoon butter or olive oil

1 small red onion, sliced

2–4oz (50–110g) chorizo, bacon, or sausages (optional)

1 red bell (sweet) pepper, sliced

5½oz (150g) cooked new potatoes, cubed

½ teaspoon smoked paprika

½ teaspoon dried chili flakes (optional)

½ cup (50g) grated Cheddar, Gouda, or Manchego cheese

Sea salt and black pepper

Writing this book has meant I've had to eat a lot of food. Thankfully, I signed up for three half-marathons during that time, so could mix long runs with long days of cooking. After one run, I got home and had some eggs in the cupboard and an open bottle of Weihenstephan Hefeweissbier on the side (before the run I'd knocked up the dough for some Beer Brioche Buns, see page 114). I couldn't resist combining them and it turned into a really great frittata (or tortilla or Spanish omelet, or whatever you want to call it)–somehow fluffier and lighter than usual. I also finished the beer while eating the frittata; it might have been 11am but I'd earned it. You can add pretty much anything you like to this: vegetables, cheese, or meat.

1 Whisk together the eggs and beer, and season with plenty of salt and black pepper. Set to one side.

2 Place the butter or oil in a deep ovenproof pan or skillet, and cook the onion for 5 minutes or until soft. If you wish, add some chorizo, bacon, or sausages and cook for 5–10 minutes, depending on what you're using.

3 Add the pepper and cook for a few more minutes, then add the potatoes and cook for a further 2–3 minutes. At this point, turn the broiler (grill) to a medium-high heat. Add the paprika (and chili flakes, if using) and some more seasoning to the pan.

4 Pour over the egg and beer mixture, stirring to ensure it fills all the gaps. Leave the frittata to cook on the stovetop, occasionally tilting the pan to ensure it cooks evenly. After a few minutes, as the sides begin to cook, scatter the cheese on top and place under the broiler (grill) for 5 minutes or until the cheese is golden and bubbling.

5 Tip the frittata onto a chopping board and allow to cool a little before serving.

BEER STYLE: HEFEWEIZEN

EAT IT WITH...

Hefeweizen is a great breakfast beer. Just go to Munich and it's as if no one even bothers with coffee and just goes straight for the wheat beer. Smooth, refreshing, yet satisfying. Weihenstephan is a favorite (or look for other classic German versions), Tröegs DreamWeaver Wheat in the US, or Burleigh Hefeweizen in Australia.

2 eggs
3 tablespoons whole milk
8 tablespoons Hefeweizen
2 tablespoons soft brown sugar
½ teaspoon each salt, ground
    nutmeg, and ground cinnamon
2 tablespoons butter, for frying
2 thick slices of fresh bread
1 banana, sliced into rings
Handful of pecan nuts
4 tablespoons maple syrup

HEFEWEIZEN FRENCH TOAST

I like eating beer for breakfast. Sure, I might not have it on a casual Tuesday morning before going to work, but it's a great start to the day on a lazy weekend. This recipe infuses traditional French toast with the soft banana flavor of Hefeweizen and is then topped off with some more banana. It's easy, quick (less than 10 minutes from bed to kitchen and then back to bed to eat it), tasty, and leaves you with most of a bottle of beer to drink while you eat.

1 Mix the eggs, milk, 4 tablespoons of the beer, sugar, salt, nutmeg, and cinnamon in a large bowl.

2 Place 1 tablespoon of butter in a large frying pan over a medium heat. Lay each slice of bread in the egg-beer mixture, allowing it to soak for a few seconds on each side, then place in the pan. Fry each slice for 2 minutes on each side or until golden brown.

3 Heat 1 tablespoon of butter in a small saucepan and add the banana rings and pecan nuts. Cook for approximately 1 minute, before adding the maple syrup, and then cook for a further minute. Remove from the heat and add the remaining 4 tablespoons of Hefeweizen.

4 Arrange the French toast on a plate and cover each slice with the banana-pecan-maple topping.

BEER STYLE: HEFEWEIZEN

EAT IT WITH...

The rest of the Hefeweizen is a good match–I always opt for Weihenstephaner because of its smooth body and creamy banana flavor. A great alternative is a Coffee Imperial Stout, one that's strong and rich, and gives the impression of drinking a boozy Americano.

BEER BRUNCH MUFFINS

MAKES 12

1 cup (225g) cottage cheese
1 cup (125g) grated Cheddar cheese
1 cup (125g) all-purpose (plain) flour
  (or go half-and-half with some
  almond flour for lighter muffins)
1 teaspoon baking powder
½ cup (75g) canned corn kernels
  (sweetcorn)
2 scallions (spring onions), finely
  chopped
1–3 green chili peppers, finely
  chopped
4 eggs, beaten
4 tablespoons Oatmeal Stout
Salt and black pepper

These corn, Cheddar cheese, chili, and Oatmeal Stout muffins make a great, healthy weekend breakfast that's quick to prepare, with the beer providing a good, roasted richness to go with the cheese and chili. These muffins work well warm or cold, and you could also add some smoked bacon.

1 Preheat the oven to 400°F/200°C/Gas 6 and line a muffin tin with some muffin cases.

2 In a large bowl, combine all of the ingredients, reserving some of the cheese. Season with salt and black pepper.

3 Spoon the mixture (which will be quite loose, so don't worry) into the muffin cases, sprinkle with the remaining cheese, and bake for 30–35 minutes.

SERVES 2

½ onion, finely chopped
1 tablespoon vegetable oil or butter,
  for frying
½ garlic clove, finely chopped
1 teaspoon sugar
Pinch of paprika
Optional extras: 2–3 rashers of
  smoked bacon (diced) or some
  dried chili flakes
14oz (400g) can chopped tomatoes
14oz (400g) can navy (haricot) beans,
  drained and rinsed
⅓ cup (100ml) Dark Beer
Dash of Worcestershire Sauce
Salt and black pepper
Thick slices of buttered toast,
  to serve

BEER BEANS ON TOAST

Because I'm English I bloody love beans on toast, a dish I grew up eating once a week. This is my grown-up, beer-enhanced version, which is even better if you use Beer Soda Bread (see page 116) to make the toast, as this gives a great additional sweetness. To keep it quick and simple, I just use canned navy (haricot) beans, but you can prepare dried beans if you prefer. I like to use a Smoked Porter in this recipe, but any rich, dark beer works well.

1 Soften the onion in the oil or butter in a saucepan for a few minutes. Add the garlic, sugar, and paprika, season with salt and black pepper, and stir for 1 minute. (Add the bacon and/or chili flakes at this stage, if using.)

2 Add the tomatoes, beans, and most of the beer (reserve around 2 tablespoons), and bring to a simmer. Allow to simmer for 10–15 minutes. Add the remaining beer and Worcestershire Sauce, check the seasoning, and then serve on thick slices of buttered toast.

BEER STYLE:
OATMEAL STOUT

EAT IT WITH...

Oatmeal Stout is a good breakfast beer, being smooth, sweet, and roasty, plus it provides the perfect flavor combination with these muffins. Try Anderson Valley's Barney Flats or St-Ambroise by McAuslan. Or, make it the ideal brunch brew with Mikkeller's Beer Geek Breakfast.

SHANDIES AND MIXERS

I'm not a fan of beer cocktails; I've never had one I'd rather drink instead of the beer on its own or a decent cocktail. Shandies are different. By adding lemonade to a lager you end up with one of the most refreshing long drinks there is—and that's crucial for me. Beer is a long drink and a shandy is refreshing, so any mixes need to adhere to those rules, whether spirits are added or not. Here are some fun shandies that require nothing more than simply stirring all the ingredients together in a glass. A couple of these can also take a shot or two of harder alcohol to give them an extra kick.

THE IPA WANNABE

¾ cup (200ml) Pale Lager, preferably
  a cheap one
¾ cup (200ml) grapefruit soda (like
  San Pellegrino)
Juice of ¼ orange

LEMON PALE SHANDY

¾ cup (200ml) Pale Ale
¾ cup (200ml) bitter lemon
Juice of ¼ grapefruit

WITBIER MIMOSA

¾ cup (200ml) Witbier
⅓ cup (100ml) fresh orange juice
⅓ cup (100ml) bitter lemon

GINGER PALE SHANDY

¾ cup (200ml) Pale Ale
¾ cup (200ml) ginger ale
Juice of ¼ lime

G&T SHANDY

1¼ cups (300ml) Pale Lager
⅔ cup (150ml) tonic water
1fl oz (25ml) gin
Juice of ½ lime

THE IPA WANNABE

Lager disguised as a Session IPA, this mixes a standard lager with grapefruit and orange to give a drink with a tangy, fruity, citrusy freshness.

LEMON PALE SHANDY

The bitter lemon adds bitterness and a refreshing sharpness, while the grapefruit gives this shandy even more aroma and a lush fruitiness.

WITBIER MIMOSA (PICTURED LEFT)

This is beer's Buck's Fizz or a refreshing breakfast drink, if you like. The Witbier naturally has a smooth orangey depth, so adding orange and lemon works very well. Gin is a good addition if you want something harder.

GINGER PALE SHANDY

Ginger ale is very nice with hops, as the spicy warmth it brings plays with the bitterness, while the addition of lime gives a slightly exotic Southeast Asian accent. Add a shot of Bourbon and a couple of dashes of bitters (grapefruit bitters are best) and it's excellent.

G&T SHANDY (PICTURED RIGHT)

This was a university favorite. We'd each order a pint of lager and a gin and tonic, down half the pint, then pour the G&T into the glass. I'm glad my career has progressed to the stage where I'm able to get this deliciousness into print. Thank you, undergraduate degree—you taught me everything I needed to become a professional drinker.

CHAPTER 2
SNACKS AND STARTERS

EAT IT WITH...

It's a beer snack, so pretty much anything and everything will be delicious, although, as the recipe uses Pale Ale, then that's a good place to start. Porter and Dunkel are also excellent.

LOADED PALE ALE POTATO SKINS

SERVES 4-6

4–8 small baking potatoes
1½ cups (200g) grated strong
   Cheddar cheese
2 tablespoons cream cheese
¼ cup (50ml) Pale Ale
1 teaspoon English or Dijon mustard
1 teaspoon onion powder
Salt and black pepper

These brilliant beer snacks are easy to make and also taste great. The combination of Pale Ale, Cheddar cheese, and mustard is always a winner, but this is really easy to adapt in different ways. Try adding some chili or cooked bacon and onion to the mix, or one of the best alternatives is to use smoked beer and smoked cheese together.

1 Preheat the oven to 400°F/200°C/Gas 6. Clean the potatoes and prick them all over with a fork. Bake in the oven for around 60–75 minutes (or until cooked through).

2 Remove the potatoes from the oven. Holding them carefully in a dish towel, cut each potato in half and scoop the insides into a bowl. Add the remaining ingredients into the bowl with the potato (reserving some of the Cheddar cheese), season with salt and black pepper, and mix together well.

3 Refill the potato skins with the potato-cheese-beer mixture and sprinkle with the reserved cheese. Return to the oven for a further 15 minutes.

FOR THE BEER-BAKED FRIES

1 bottle of Porter or IPA
3 tablespoons salt
2 tablespoons sugar
Lots of black pepper
Rosemary sprig
A few whole garlic cloves
1–2 potatoes, per person (unpeeled)
Olive oil, for baking

FOR THE HOP SALT

1 hop pellet or flower
2–3 tablespoons sea salt

FOR THE WEIZEN KETCHUP
MAKES 4 X 1LB (450G) JARS

1 large red onion, finely diced
Olive oil, for frying
18oz (500g) fresh tomatoes, quartered
2 x 14oz (400g) cans plum tomatoes
3 garlic cloves, roughly chopped
2 red chili peppers, finely chopped
1 cup (200g) brown sugar
¾ cup (200ml) wheat beer
⅓ cup (100ml) malt vinegar
½ bunch of fresh basil leaves
1 teaspoon each fresh thyme leaves,
    ground cinnamon, fennel seeds,
    onion powder, and cayenne pepper
Salt and black pepper

BEER STYLE:
ANYTHING

EAT IT WITH...
It's a beer snack, so pretty much anything and everything will be delicious, although, as the recipe uses a Porter or IPA, then that's a good place to start.

BEER-BAKED FRIES
WITH HOP SALT AND WEIZEN KETCHUP

This recipe uses beer as a brine for the fries, seasons them with hop salt, and puts beer-infused ketchup on the side. For the brine, I've experimented with Porter and IPA, with the Porter giving a subtle additional sweetness that complements the cooking process and the IPA kicking out some bitterness.

1 Pour the beer into a large bowl and add the salt, sugar, and black pepper. Stir well until all the ingredients are combined. Add the sprig of rosemary and garlic (or whichever additional flavors you prefer).

2 Cut the potatoes into the shape of fries you like best–fat, thin, whatever–and add them to the beer brine. Top up with cool water so that all the potatoes are covered. Cover with plastic wrap (clingfilm) and leave for 1–4 hours in the refrigerator.

3 To cook the fries, preheat the oven to 400°F/200°C/Gas 6. Remove the fries from the beer brine, dry off the liquid with some paper towel, and then spread them out on a baking tray. Drizzle the fries with oil, tossing them well to ensure they are evenly coated. Season the fries with more salt and pepper.

4 Bake the fries in the oven for 30–45 minutes, depending on the size of your fry cut.

TO MAKE THE HOP SALT

Take a hop pellet or flower, and crumble off a small amount (literally very small). Grind this in a pestle and mortar, and then mix with the sea salt. Taste it: if it's too bitter, add more salt. A quicker alternative is to put some sea salt in a small container with a lid and add one whole hop flower, which will infuse the salt with its hoppy flavor.

TO MAKE THE KETCHUP

1 This can be made months in advance or you can cook it fresh. To make, gently soften the onion in some olive oil in a large saucepan over a medium heat.

2 Add the fresh and canned tomatoes to the onion, along with the garlic cloves and chili peppers, stirring and cooking for 10 minutes. Add the remaining ingredients, season with salt and black pepper, put the lid on the pan, simmer for 60 minutes, and then for a further 30 minutes with the lid off. Allow the ketchup to cool before blitzing into a smooth sauce in a blender. Transfer the ketchup to sterilized jars (see page 4).

ORVAL RILLETTES

Pork fat and beer. That's the essence of this recipe, which is pork belly slow-cooked until it melts into itself before being placed in jars, topped off with its own fat—basically reconstructing it—then chilled until it turns thick enough to spread on toast. Of course, it's not healthy, but it's damn tasty (think of it as pulled pork set in pork fat) and the beer gives a great nudge of pepper and citrus. Alternative styles to the Orval include Saison or Bière de Garde. Serve with toast (Beer Soda Bread is good, so see page 116) and something sweet and sharp such as Snakebite Pickles (see page 36) or Beer Chutney (see page 43). My mate Matt cooked this recipe and it was so good it made the book.

SERVES 8-10

2¼lb (1kg) pork belly, skinned, boned, and cut into 2in (5cm) cubes

3½oz (100g) pork fat, cut into 2in (5cm) cubes

1 tablespoon sea salt

1 tablespoon white pepper

1 teaspoon five spice

1 tablespoon brown sugar

1 bottle of Orval (or other blonde beer)

4 bay leaves

Large thyme sprig

4 whole garlic cloves

Zest of ½ lemon (use a peeler so that it stays in large strips)

1 Preheat the over to 275°F/140°C/Gas 1. Place the pork and fat in a lidded roasting pan and rub with the salt, white pepper, five spice, and sugar.

2 Pour the beer into the roasting pan along with the remaining ingredients. Place the lid on the pan and roast in the oven for 3 hours or until the pork is melting and soft.

3 Remove the pan from the oven and place the pork in a large bowl. Use a pair of forks to shred the meat (as if you're making pulled pork). Put the meat into individual ramekins.

4 Pour the liquid remaining in the roasting pan through a sieve into a pouring jug to remove the bay leaves, thyme sprig, garlic cloves, and lemon.

5 Pour the strained liquid over the pork and leave to cool before refrigerating, ideally for a few days (but at least overnight). It'll last in the refrigerator for a week or so.

BEER STYLE:
BELGIAN BLONDE

EAT IT WITH...

Orval is a great choice, with its bitterness cutting through the fat, but any good Belgian Blonde or Pale Ale works well, especially one with a lift of bright carbonation and dry bitterness such as Brasserie de la Senne's Taras Boulba, St Bernardus Extra 4, or even something a little sharp like De Brabandere Petrus Aged Pale.

SNAKEBITE PICKLES

The student's drink of choice, Snakebite is an equal mix of lager and cider, which is a fast-forward to happy drunkenness. Adapted here, it becomes the base for pickled vegetables that are perfect with strong cheese, on the side of barbecue dishes, or just straight from the jar as a snack. You can choose whatever vegetables you want, which makes this recipe versatile, and add any seasoning you like. I like celery, classic pickled cucumbers, carrots, and chili peppers (sometimes all together in one jar) and use a decent bittersweet lager such as Pilsner Urquell, but Pale Ale and IPA are also really good options here.

SERVES MANY

MAKES 1 X 1¾ PINTS (1 LITER)
KILNER JAR

1¼ cups (300ml) cider vinegar
¾ cup (200ml) water
½ cup (100g) Demerara sugar
¼ cup (50g) superfine (caster) sugar
1oz (25g) sea salt
2¼lb (1kg) vegetables of choice (such as celery, carrots, etc.)
1 cup (250ml) Pale Lager (or Pale Ale)

Optional extras: 1 teaspoon each coriander seeds and/or peppercorns, dried chili flakes, fennel seeds, dill, etc. (my favorite combo is simply coriander seeds and peppercorns)

1 Add the cider vinegar, water, sugars, sea salt, and spices (if using) to a saucepan. Bring to a boil and stir for around 5 minutes until the sugar and salt dissolve. Turn off the heat.

2 Take a large sterilized Kilner jar (see page 4 for guidance on sterilizing). Prepare the vegetables by peeling (if necessary), chopping them into a shape that will best fit the jar (long and thin is good), and then pack them in as tightly as possible.

3 Pour the beer into the vinegar mix in the pan and then pour this carefully into the jar, filling it with as much liquid as possible.

4 Seal the jar, allow to cool, and then place in the refrigerator for a couple of days. The pickles will stay good for a few weeks.

FRAMBOISE AND HAZELNUT DRESSING

1fl oz (25ml) Framboise
1fl oz (25ml) balsamic vinegar
1fl oz (25ml) hazelnut oil

STOUT AND BALSAMIC VINEGAR DRESSING WITH CHILI FLAKES

1fl oz (25ml) Stout
1fl oz (25ml) balsamic vinegar
2fl oz (50ml) peppery olive oil
Dried chili flakes

HONEY MUSTARD AND IPA DRESSING

1 teaspoon honey
1 teaspoon wholegrain mustard
1 teaspoon fresh orange juice
1fl oz (25ml) IPA
2fl oz (50ml) olive oil

BARLEY WINE, HONEY, AND WALNUT OIL DRESSING

1fl oz (25ml) Barley Wine
1 tablespoon honey
2fl oz (50ml) walnut oil

FOUR GREAT BEER SALAD DRESSINGS

The acidity or bitterness in beer can create excellent salad dressings, and you'll also keep all the great beer aroma because you aren't cooking it. I typically shake up these dressings in an empty glass jar with a lid. Here are four great beer salads, plus some additional serving suggestions:

FRAMBOISE AND HAZELNUT DRESSING WITH GOATS' CHEESE, BEETS (BEETROOT), AND HAZELNUTS

Combine the Framboise, vinegar, and hazelnut oil in a glass jar with a lid. Pour over goats' cheese, beets (beetroot), roasted hazelnuts, and some peppery salad leaves such as arugula (rocket).

STOUT AND BALSAMIC VINEGAR DRESSING WITH CHILI FLAKES

Pour the Stout, vinegar, and olive oil into a glass jar with a lid, add some chili flakes and shake to mix. Serve with steak and a side salad.

HONEY MUSTARD AND IPA DRESSING WITH ROAST PORK OR CHICKEN

Add all the ingredients to a jar with a lid and combine. Serve with roast pork or chicken and a side salad.

BARLEY WINE, HONEY, AND WALNUT OIL DRESSING OVER HOT FIGS, BLUE CHEESE, AND PROSCIUTTO

To make the dressing, add the Barley Wine, honey, and walnut oil to a jar with a lid and shake well to combine. To make the hot figs, slice a cross in the top, and stuff in some blue cheese. Wrap it all in prosciutto. You'll want 3–5 wrapped figs per person. Bake the figs in the oven for 10 minutes at 400°F/200°C/Gas 6. Serve the figs on a bed of salad leaves, sprinkled with walnuts, and drizzled with the salad dressing.

SERVES 4

FOR THE BEER HOT WINGS

1 bottle of Pale Ale or IPA
3 tablespoons sugar
3 tablespoons salt
3 garlic cloves, chopped
1 tablespoon dried chili flakes
1 tablespoon paprika
12 black peppercorns
2¼lb (1kg) chicken wings

TO COOK: salt, black pepper, chili powder or flakes, onion powder, and garlic powder

FOR THE HOT SAUCE
MAKES 2 X 15FL OZ (450ML) JARS

6–8 peaches, stoned and halved
2–4 habanero chili peppers (adjust to suit your love of heat), chopped
1 onion, chopped
4 whole garlic cloves
2 tablespoons olive oil
4 tablespoons sugar
Zest and juice of 1 orange
Scant 1 cup (230ml) cider vinegar
½ cup (125ml) Pale Ale or IPA
Salt and black pepper

FOR THE BLUE CHEESE DIP

½ cup (100g) cream cheese
½ cup (100g) full fat natural yogurt
3½oz (100g) blue cheese, crumbled
¼ cup (50ml) Milk or Oatmeal Stout

BEER HOT WINGS
WITH HOPPY PEACH HOT SAUCE AND BEER BLUE CHEESE DIP

Do you like hot wings? Do you like beer? Then this is the perfect dish for you, because it uses beer in every element of the ultimate beer snack platter. The wings are brined and you can use most beers for this. They will pick up some bitterness if you use Pale Ale or IPA and I enjoy that.

TO MAKE THE BEER HOT WINGS

1 Begin a day in advance to make the brine. In a large sealable container mix the bottle of beer with an equal amount of cold water. Add the sugar and salt and stir until combined. Add the garlic, chili flakes, paprika, and peppercorns. Add the chicken wings to the brine, put the lid on, and place in the refrigerator for 12–24 hours.

2 Preheat the oven to 425°F/220°C/Gas7–I like to bake my hot wings. Remove the chicken wings from the brine and pat them dry with some paper towel. Place in a bowl and add more seasoning, including pinches of chili powder or flakes, onion powder, and garlic powder. Place the wings on a baking tray and cook in the oven for 30 minutes, or until crisp and golden on the outside and cooked in the middle. Tip into a bowl and either pour over the hot sauce or pop this in a separate dish for dipping. Serve the beer blue cheese dip on the side.

TO MAKE THE HOPPY PEACH HOT SAUCE

1 This can be made days or weeks in advance, with the flavor improving over time. To begin, preheat the oven to 400°F/200°C/Gas 6. Place the peaches, chili peppers, onion, and garlic on a baking tray, drizzle with the olive oil, and cook in the oven for 20 minutes.

2 Transfer the peaches to a saucepan. Add the remaining ingredients, apart from the beer, season with salt and pepper, and simmer for 20 minutes. Remove from the heat and allow to cool. Pour in the beer and blitz everything in a blender until you have a thick sauce. Taste the sauce to see if it's hot enough– you can always add more raw chilis at this stage and continue blending. Transfer to sterilized jars (see page 4).

TO MAKE THE BEER BLUE CHEESE DIP

1 In a blender, combine all the ingredients and pulse until it creates a thick sauce.

EAT IT WITH...

I like smooth dark beers like Oatmeal and Milk Stouts, as they love spice and keep everything cool and under control. Left Hand Nitro Milk Stout is a favorite of mine; Summer Wine Mokko Milk Stout and Nail Brewing Oatmeal Stout are also superb.

EAT IT WITH...

A good English Bitter, ESB, Porter, or Stout. The toasty malt flavor is great with herby sausages, plus it can handle the sharp-sweetness of the chutney. Fuller's ESB or London Porter would be ideal choices.

FOR THE SCOTCH EGGS

6 eggs

⅓ cup (100ml) Porter

14oz (400g) sausage meat (or use
  good-quality sausages with the
  skins removed)

Selection of herbs and spices (I like
  to use fresh thyme and sage,
  onion powder, ½ teaspoon of
  English mustard, and a pinch
  of cayenne pepper)

1¼ cups (75g) fresh breadcrumbs

1oz (25g) packet of potato chips
  (I like to use cheese and onion)

1oz (25g) salted peanuts

Scant ½ cup (50g) all-purpose
  (plain) flour, plus extra for
  dusting

8½ cups (2 liters) vegetable oil
  (optional, if deep-frying)

Salt and black pepper

FOR THE BEER CHUTNEY
MAKES 2 X 1LB (450G) JARS

2–3 tablespoons olive oil, for frying

2 large red onions, thinly sliced

1 large carrot, cut into ½in (1cm)
  cubes

1 zucchini (courgette), cut into ½in
  (1cm) cubes

1 cooked beet (beetroot), cut into
  ½in (1cm) cubes

1 large cooking apple, peeled,
  cored, and diced

⅓ cup (50g) raisins or dried
  apricots

1 tablespoon mustard seeds

1 teaspoon ground coriander

½ teaspoon cayenne pepper

1 tablespoon Worcestershire sauce

1 cup (200g) light muscovado sugar

½ cup (125ml) malt vinegar

½ cup (125ml) Porter or Stout

Salt and black pepper

SCOTCH EGGS
WITH BEER CHUTNEY

Scotch eggs are a top bar snack... as are potato chips and
peanuts. Here, they are combined in one ultimate beer snack,
which also includes some Porter in the recipe.

1 To make the Scotch eggs, place four of the eggs in a saucepan of
boiling water. Set a timer for 6 minutes. Remove the eggs from
the pan and place in cold water. When cooled, peel the eggs,
put them in a small bowl or sandwich bag, and pour over
6 tablespoons of the Porter. Leave the eggs to soak for a few
minutes until you're ready.

2 Put the sausage meat in a bowl and add 3 tablespoons of the
Porter, as well as the herbs and spices, and some seasoning–you
can freestyle a bit here, depending on which flavors you want.
Divide the sausage mixture into four equal balls.

3 Blitz the breadcrumbs, potato chips, and peanuts in a blender
until you have a very fine mix to coat the balls of sausage meat.

4 Set up an assembly line of three bowls: put the flour in one, the
remaining two eggs (beaten) in the second, and the breadcrumb
mix in the third.

5 Dust your hands with some flour and take a ball of sausage
meat, squashing it flat. Place an egg in the middle and wrap
everything into a ball. Roll the ball in the flour, then in the egg,
and then cover with breadcrumbs. Set to one side and repeat
for the other eggs.

6 To cook, either bake for 30 minutes in the oven (preheated
to 400°F/200°C/Gas 6) or deep-fry in vegetable oil at 325°F
(170°C) for about 7 minutes. Allow to cool slightly (or fully)
before serving.

TO MAKE THE BEER CHUTNEY

1 Heat the olive oil in a large saucepan and slowly cook the
onions for about 10 minutes, or until they are soft and sweet.

2 Add the carrot, zucchini (courgette), beet (beetroot), apple, and
dried fruit, followed by the rest of the ingredients. Bring to a
simmer, then cook for 60–90 minutes, or until the chutney has
reduced and thickened.

3 Spoon the chutney into sterilized jars (see page 4) and store until
needed (the flavor improves over time).

BEER CHILI BUNS

This is what happens if you combine the disparate influences of dim sum, chili, burgers, and a Cornish pasty. Basically it's a baked, stuffed bread roll that makes an awesome beer snack. It uses a beer-cooked chili as the filling–the best choice here is a strong, rich Stout or Imperial Stout. The bread also includes beer, with Stout and Oatmeal Stout being the best choice; just avoid hop bitterness.

MAKES 12

FOR THE BEER CHILI

9oz (250g) ground (minced) beef or pork
1 tablespoon olive oil, for frying
1 onion, finely chopped
1 carrot, finely chopped
1–3 chili peppers (depending on your heat preference), finely chopped
1 garlic clove, finely chopped
1 tablespoon tomato paste (purée)
1 teaspoon each brown sugar, smoked paprika, chili powder, ground cumin, and salt and black pepper
Pinch of ground cinnamon
1/3 cup (100ml) hot beef stock
1 bottle of Stout

FOR THE BEER BUNS

4 tablespoons warm water
1 x 1/4oz (7g) sachet fast-action dried yeast
1 tablespoon sugar
1/3 cup (100ml) Stout
Scant 2½ cups (330g) strong white bread flour, plus extra for dusting
1 teaspoon salt
7 tablespoons (100g) butter, at room temperature
1 beaten egg, to glaze

1 To make the chili filling, brown the ground (minced) beef or pork in the olive oil in a large saucepan or flameproof casserole dish for 5 minutes. Add the onion, carrot, chili peppers, garlic, and tomato paste (purée) and stir together for another 5 minutes.

2 Add all the spices and seasoning, followed by the stock, and then the beer. Place a lid on the pan or casserole dish, and either cook on the stovetop or in the oven (at 325°F/160°C/Gas 3) for up to 2 hours, until the chili is thick and there is no liquid left. When the chili is cooked, set to one side to cool. (The chili can be made a day or two in advance and kept in the refrigerator.)

3 To make the buns, pour the warm water into a mixing jug or cup with the yeast and sugar. Leave for 2 minutes and then add the beer.

4 In a large bowl, combine the flour and salt, and then rub in the butter with your fingers until the mixture resembles breadcrumbs. Add the yeast liquid and use your hands to bring everything together until you have a thick dough. Remove the dough from the bowl, dust some flour on the work surface, and knead the dough for 5 minutes.

5 Cut the dough into 12 equal balls and place on a large tray with space between them. Leave the dough balls in a warm, dry place to prove for an hour.

6 Preheat the oven to 350°F/180°C/Gas 4. Place some baking paper on a large baking tray. Take a dough ball and flatten it using your hand or a rolling pin. Place a large scoop of beer chili in the middle and wrap into a ball. Turn the ball over so that the seal sits on the baking tray (just make sure there isn't too much dough folded at the base or you'll get an uneven bake). Repeat for all the dough balls. Glaze with the beaten egg. Bake for 20–25 minutes until golden brown. Eat warm or cold.

RECIPE VARIATIONS:

How about filling the balls with a beer-tomato sauce, fresh basil, and a ball of mozzarella? Or be inspired by a cheeseburger: make a mixture of ground (minced) beef, onions, beer, ketchup, mustard, and seasoning and then place some burger cheese inside when you make the buns and sprinkle them with sesame seeds before baking.

EAT IT WITH...

Whatever beer you're drinking, as these are beer snacks.
The best flavor combinations will come from Golden Ales,
Dark Lagers, or Hefeweizen, which love spice and bread.

MEXICAN LAGER AND CORN SOUP

1 white onion, finely chopped

Olive oil or butter, for frying

½ teaspoon sugar

2 garlic cloves, finely chopped

1–2 green chili peppers, finely chopped

½ teaspoon smoked paprika

2½–2¾ cups (350–400g) corn kernels (sweetcorn) (either fresh, canned, or frozen)

1 avocado, skinned, stoned, and diced

⅔ cup (150ml) hot chicken or vegetable stock

1 bottle of Mexican lager

Juice of 1 lime

Salt and black pepper

Handful of fresh cilantro (coriander), to serve

There are times when you have beer that you don't really want to drink. Say, for example, that a "friend" brought over a six-pack of horrible Mexican lager—you know: the sort of beer that needs lime in the neck to make it taste even slightly acceptable. You don't want to drink that, but you don't want to just throw it away either. So, here's a way to turn that tasteless lager into a simple soup (which handily also works as a morning-after reviver).

1 Soften the onion in a little olive oil or butter in a saucepan. Add the sugar, stirring slowly for 5 minutes as it begins to caramelize. Add the garlic and chili pepper, stirring for a couple of minutes, and then the paprika.

2 Add most of the corn kernels (sweetcorn), reserving ⅓–⅔ cup (50–100g), followed by the avocado.

3 Pour in the stock and then the beer, and simmer for 10 minutes.

4 Transfer the mixture to a blender and blitz until smooth. Add the lime juice and check the seasoning, adding salt, black pepper, or more chili pepper, as required.

5 Mix in the remaining corn kernels (sweetcorn) and serve with fresh cilantro (coriander) on the side. This soup is great served with Lager Tacos (see page 77).

BEER STYLE: WHEAT BEER

EAT IT WITH...

Go for a smooth, creamy wheat beer (either hoppy or subtle), such as Sierra Nevada Kellerweiss or Boulevard 80 Acre Hoppy Wheat, or a classic like Weihenstephaner Hefe Weissbier.

CURRIED BUTTERNUT SQUASH AND PORTER SOUP

SERVES 2-4

1 large butternut squash, peeled and deseeded (reserve the seeds)

1 tablespoon cooking oil

2 tablespoons curry powder (or your own mix of ground coriander, ground cumin, ground turmeric, chili powder, ground ginger, and a pinch of ground cinnamon)

Smoked paprika (optional)

3 garlic cloves

1–3 chili peppers (depending on your heat preference)

Olive oil, for drizzling

2 onions, finely chopped

Butter or mild cooking oil (olive oil is perfect)

2 cups (500ml) hot chicken or vegetable stock

1 bottle of Porter

Salt and black pepper

Crème fraîche, to serve (optional)

This is a kind of meal-soup that's perfect for warming you up on a cold day. The addition of Porter—choose something rich and smooth—gives the soup an extra warming depth and also enhances the roasted qualities of the baked butternut squash.

1 Preheat the oven to 350°F/180°C/Gas 4.

2 Start by separating out the squash seeds. If the seeds still have some pulp around them, place them in a colander and rinse this off. Pat the seeds dry with some paper towel and spread them out on a baking tray with a tablespoon of cooking oil. Season with salt and black pepper. (You can also add extra chili powder, as well as some smoked paprika, if you wish.)

3 Chop the squash into large chunks (around 1in/2cm cubed) and place on a second baking tray with the garlic cloves and chili peppers. Drizzle with olive oil. Sprinkle the squash with a teaspoon each of salt and black pepper, plus the curry powder, and mix well so the squash is covered with seasoning. Place the trays of squash and seeds in the oven for 30 minutes, turning the contents of each once during cooking.

4 Meanwhile, sweat the onion in some butter or cooking oil in a saucepan—you want the onions to be soft and sweet, so cook them for 10–15 minutes, making sure that they don't burn.

5 When the squash and seeds are cooked, remove them from the oven. Set the seeds to one side. Add the squash (including the garlic cloves and chili peppers) to the onion in the pan and stir for 1 minute. Pour in the stock and most of the beer, reserving ¼ cup (50ml). Simmer for 10 minutes.

6 Remove from the heat and blitz to a thick, smooth soup in a blender. Add the remaining beer, taste, and adjust the seasoning, as required.

7 Pour the soup into bowls, adding a spoon of crème fraîche to each bowl (if desired). Finish by sprinkling the squash seeds on top. Serve with some fresh bread.

BEER STYLE: PORTER

EAT IT WITH...

Porter is the ideal choice (especially the beer that you used in the recipe). Try Great Lakes Edmund Fitzgerald Porter, Harviestoun's Old Engine Oil, or Bridge Road Robust Porter.

SERVES 4

½ red onion, finely chopped

9oz (250g) fresh white fish, cut
    into ½in (1cm) cubes

½ red chili pepper

Juice of 1 lime

¼ cup (50ml) Sour Beer

½ teaspoon sea salt

½ teaspoon ground coriander

2 avocados, skinned, stoned, and
    sliced, to serve

Handful of fresh cilantro
    (coriander), to serve

SOUR BEER CEVICHE

Recipes don't get much simpler than this and yet its simplicity belies the excellence of this acidic, refreshing, Peruvian-inspired dish. The fish–a white fish like sea bass is best–is quickly cured using the acidity of citrus and sour beer, where Gueuze will give a tangy, peppery edge; modern "quick" sours (the Berliner-Weisse style) will give a tart, lactic edge; and a fruited sour adds in a nice bonus burst of flavor. Just make sure the fish is the freshest you can buy.

1 Soak the onion in some iced water for 10 minutes to take the harsher edge off the flavor.

2 Meanwhile, place the fish in a large serving bowl. Add all the other ingredients, apart from the avocado and cilantro (coriander), and mix together gently. Leave to cure in the refrigerator for 30–60 minutes. Check the seasoning (adding more salt or citrus, if you prefer).

3 To serve, place the fish on top of the sliced avocado and sprinkle with cilantro (coriander).

BEER STYLE:
SOUR BEER

EAT IT WITH...
The sour beer you cured the fish in works best, where something such as Girardin is a nice choice for its balance of acidity and subtle sweetness. A good alternative is a cold dark lager–try something simple like Negra Modelo or a classic German version.

3 tablespoons coriander seeds
1 teaspoon fennel seeds
1 tablespoon white pepper
   (or peppercorns)
⅔ cup (200g) sea salt
1½ cups (300g) Demerara sugar
Zest of 1 lemon and 2 oranges
1 filleted side of salmon (as fresh
   as possible)
1 bottle of Witbier

WITBIER-CURED SALMON

This uses ground coriander, citrus zest, and white pepper to infuse and cure a side of salmon with the flavors of a classic Witbier, where the beer also gets used and soaks into the fish. Just make sure that you get the freshest fish possible from your fishmonger.

1 Toast the coriander and fennel seeds (plus the peppercorns, if using) in a dry pan for a few minutes before crushing in a pestle and mortar. Place in a large bowl and mix in the salt, sugar, white pepper (if you haven't used peppercorns instead), and citrus zest.

2 Place the salmon fillet, skin side down, on a large piece of aluminum foil (this needs to be at least three times larger than the fish).

3 Pour approximately 5 tablespoons (75ml) of the beer into a cup or bowl (cover the beer bottle and put it in the refrigerator, you'll need it in a day or two). Brush the salmon on both sides with some of the beer, leaving the rest in the cup for a moment.

4 Cover the salmon in the salt-sugar mix, rubbing it in well and ensuring that both sides are completely covered. Gently pour over the remainder of the beer in the cup and rub it into the fish.

5 Wrap the salmon tightly in the foil and then again in plastic wrap (clingfilm). Place the salmon on a large tray and put in the refrigerator. Put another tray on top and weigh it down (I use beer cans for this). Refrigerate for 12 hours.

6 Open up the foil, drain off the excess liquid, and wrap the salmon up again. Refrigerate for another 12 hours, and then open, drain, and reseal the foil parcel as before. Repeat this process, leaving the salmon to cure for a total of 36–48 hours.

7 An hour before you want to eat it, unwrap the salmon and slowly pour over the remaining Witbier to wash off the salt-sugar cure. Dry off with some paper towel. If there's any beer left, brush a small amount over the salmon and then place uncovered in the refrigerator.

8 To serve, finely slice the salmon and eat with a simple salad of finely sliced fresh fennel and a dressing made from fresh orange juice, fresh lemon juice, olive oil, a splash of Witbier (if you have any left), and a pinch of ground coriander.

BEER STYLE: WITBIER

EAT IT WITH...

This dish is based on the flavors of the beer and works perfectly with it, highlighting the coriander and the orange in the beer. St. Bernardus Wit is a great choice and the classic Hoegaarden works very well, as does Allagash White.

EAT IT WITH...

I like these pies best with a good glass of Stout or Porter. Try Anchor Porter, Samuel Smith Taddy Porter, or 4 Pines Stout.

MINI BEEF AND BEER PIES

This is classic beer cooking that's probably been around for centuries. A beef and beer pie is the type of dish that was made for convenience and cheapness: there would have been pots of beer in the kitchen; there were cuts of meat that needed slow-cooking; pastry was cheap and easy to prepare; and together those humble ingredients created a delicious dinner. This version puts beer in the pie (shortcrust) pastry, as well as in the meat filling. It works for snack-sized versions, but you can easily make one large pie (you may just need to add 10 minutes to the cooking time). You can make the pastry and the filling in advance. And, for the beer choice, there's just one simple rule: if you can taste hops, then don't bother using it. Belgian Dubbel is great, as is a smooth Porter or a malty Brown Ale.

MAKES 10-12

FOR THE PIE FILLING

18oz (500g) chuck (braising) steak, cubed
2 tablespoons all-purpose (plain) flour
Olive oil, for frying
2 white onions, sliced
2 carrots, cut into small cubes
1 garlic clove, finely chopped
1 tablespoon tomato paste (purée)
1 teaspoon sugar
¾ cup (200ml) hot beef stock
1⅔ cup (400ml) Dark Beer
2 bay leaves
1 tablespoon fresh thyme leaves
Salt and black pepper

FOR THE PIE (SHORTCRUST) PASTRY

Scant 2½ cups (300g) all-purpose (plain) flour
1 teaspoon salt
1¼ sticks (150g) butter (at room temperature), plus extra for greasing
2-4 tablespoons very cold Dark Beer
1 beaten egg, to glaze

1 Preheat the oven to 300°F/150°C/Gas 2.

2 To make the pie filling, toss the steak in the flour and plenty of salt and black pepper. Add a few splashes of olive oil to a large flameproof casserole dish (choose one that fits both the oven and stovetop), and brown the steak on all sides on the stovetop. Remove the steak from the dish and set to one side.

3 Add the onion and carrots to the dish and cook for a couple of minutes. Add the garlic, tomato paste (purée), and sugar. Cook for about 5 minutes, stirring constantly.

4 Return the steak to the dish, pour in the beef stock and beer, and add the bay and thyme leaves. Put the lid on the dish, bring to a gentle simmer, and transfer to the oven to cook for up to 2 hours, checking every hour or so until the filling is nice and thick–you want it to be quite dry and not like a stew. Remove the dish from the oven and set to one side to cool. You can keep the filling in the refrigerator for a day or two before making the pies.

5 To make the pastry, combine the flour and salt in a large bowl, and then use your hands to rub the butter into the flour until the mixture resembles breadcrumbs. Add the beer–make sure it's cold–a tablespoon at a time and combine until you have a pastry dough. Wrap the dough in plastic wrap (clingfilm) and place in the refrigerator for at least 30 minutes (it'll be fine in there for a day if you're making it in advance).

6 To cook the pies, preheat the oven to 400°F/200°C/Gas 6. Roll out the pastry until it's ⅛–¼in (3–5mm) thick. Cut out circles of pastry and push them into a buttered muffin tray. Spoon in the filling and place another smaller circle of pastry on top of each pie. Crimp the pie edges and cut a small cross in the top of each. Glaze with the beaten egg. Bake in the oven for 30–35 minutes or until golden brown. The pies are great eaten warm or cold.

BEER FISH FINGER SANDWICH

Batter is one of the best-known ways to use beer in the kitchen. The bubbles in the lager, plus the sweetness, combine to give a light, crisp coating. The actual batter recipe is very simple and can easily be adapted depending on what you're deep-frying (and you can deep-fry a lot of things). Here's a classic beer batter for making fish fingers and creating my favorite sandwich.

SERVES 4

Oil, for frying (sunflower oil is fine)

FOR THE BEER-BATTERED FISH FINGERS

1¾ cups (225g) all-purpose (plain) flour, plus a little extra for dusting
3 teaspoons baking powder
Generous 1 cup (275ml) very cold lager
4 white fish fillets, each cut into 4 fat strips
Sea salt and black pepper

FOR THE SANDWICH, PER PERSON

4 fish fingers
2 thick slices of fresh white bread
Butter
Ketchup

1 Heat the oil in a deep-fat fryer or large pan to 350°F (180°C). Test that the oil has reached temperature using a cooking thermometer. (You can also drop a chunk of bread or potato in the oil to test this instead—if it sizzles and browns, then the temperature is about right.)

2 To make the beer batter, mix together the flour, baking powder, and 1 teaspoon of sea salt, then whisk in the cold beer until you have a thick mix.

3 Have the fish fillets ready to go. Season the fish with salt and black pepper, dust in a little flour, then cover in the batter and lower into the hot oil. Cook the fillets for around 4–5 minutes until crisp and golden. Remove from the oil and drain on some paper towel.

4 When assembling the sandwiches, you could use some Classic Beer Bread (see page 112) and add some Weizen Ketchup (see page 34), but I don't think you need to complicate this. Butter the bread, put the hot fish fingers on top of the first slice, squeeze on some ketchup, and press down on the top slice of bread. It's hard to better this sandwich!

BEER STYLE:
PILSNER OR GOLDEN ALE

EAT IT WITH...

Something refreshing and light and fruity with hops. A modern, well-hopped Pilsner is a good choice, such as Camden Town Brewery's Pils, or go for a vibrant Golden Ale like St Austell's Tribute, Salopian Oracle, or Mountain Goat Summer Ale.

HOPCORN **CHICKEN**

In Vietnam one of the best street-side snacks to go with the glasses of cool Bia Hoi beer are the little nuggets of fried chicken served with hot sauce (which are surprisingly similar to the popcorn chicken you can get in fast-food joints). These go from popcorn to hopcorn by being brined in IPA and then deep-fried. This is my ideal kind of beer snack and you can use any IPA you like in the brine.

SERVES 4–6

1 quantity of beer brine (see recipe for the Beer Hot Wings brine on page 40 as a guide)

3 whole star anise or 1 teaspoon five spice

6–8 boneless and skinless chicken thighs, diced into 1in (2.5cm) cubes

Oil (such as peanut, vegetable, or sunflower oil), for frying

Scant ½ cup (50g) all-purpose (plain) flour

2 teaspoons salt

2 teaspoons black pepper

1 teaspoon each cayenne pepper, freshly ground coriander seeds, and onion powder

1 Prepare the brine in a large bowl, following the recipe instructions on page 40, but replacing the paprika with 3 star anise or 1 teaspoon of five spice.

2 Place the small chunks of chicken in the bowl, cover, and place in the refrigerator to marinate for 4–24 hours.

3 When you're ready to cook, remove the chicken from the brine and dry it well using some paper towels. Heat plenty of oil in a large pan (a deep-fat fryer is better, but a pan is fine). The oil should reach a temperature of about 350°F (180°C). Check this by placing a small piece of chicken in the oil–it should sizzle immediately and turn golden within a few minutes.

4 Combine the flour, salt and pepper, and remaining spices in a bowl.

5 Coat the chicken in the seasoned flour and fry for 3–4 minutes in small batches, turning carefully and occasionally. When cooked, drain on some paper towel and then eat with some hot sauce on the side.

BEER STYLE:
PALE ALE

EAT IT WITH...
You want the cooling refreshment of a Pale Ale or Lager with these. Anything cold and fresh is ideal and no single beer is better than another since everything is good.

CHAPTER 3
MAINS AND MORE

BOILERMAKER RIBS
WITH DIPA SLAW AND IPA CORNBREAD

FOR THE BOILERMAKER RIBS

1 tablespoon each sea salt, black pepper, brown sugar, smoked paprika, and ground coriander

1 teaspoon each dried chili flakes, English mustard powder, and five spice

2 racks of baby back ribs

2 red onions, peeled and quartered

4 garlic cloves

4 tablespoons soy sauce

2 tablespoons hot sauce

2 tablespoons malt vinegar

2 bottles of Stout, preferably a big strong one

4fl oz (100ml) Bourbon

FOR THE DIPA MAYONNAISE

2 egg yolks

1 teaspoon Dijon mustard

Pinch of salt

¾ cup (200ml) oil (preferably something neutral)

1 tablespoon cider vinegar

2 tablespoons Double IPA

FOR THE SLAW

3 tablespoons DIPA mayonnaise

1 tablespoon crème fraîche

1 tablespoon fresh orange juice

1 tablespoon cider vinegar

2 carrots, grated

¼ white cabbage, shredded

¼ red cabbage, shredded

Sea salt, black pepper, and ground coriander, to season

TWO CHOICES HERE: you can either make your own mayo, or cheat and use ready-made. If you go ready-made, then follow from the slaw part of the recipe (Step 2) and add 2 tablespoons of beer and 1 teaspoon of Dijon mustard to 3 tablespoons of ready-made mayo.

If you slow-cook ribs in Stout and Bourbon you get the beer's roasted richness and then the sweetly spicy flavor of the Bourbon infusing the ribs with more depth. It's the kind of recipe that's easy to put together, requiring minimal effort and giving you plenty of drinking time, but which turns out terrifically tasty. The slaw is punchy with DIPA mayonnaise, while the cornbread (see page 115 for recipe) is bittersweet with IPA and honey.

TO MAKE THE RIBS

1 Combine all the dry ingredients (the salt, spices, and sugar, etc.) in a bowl.

2 Place the ribs in a large ovenproof dish with a lid—you want the ribs to fit the dish nicely, so you may need to cut them down. Rub the spice mix into the ribs, then add the onion and garlic to the dish. Put the lid on the dish and place in the refrigerator for 2 hours.

3 Combine the remaining liquid ingredients in a jug and pour over the ribs. Keep the ribs in the refrigerator for a further 2–12 hours, removing them an hour or two before you cook.

4 Preheat the oven to 325°F/160°C/Gas 3 and cook the ribs with the lid on for 1½–2 hours, spooning the juices over them occasionally and ensuring they don't bubble dry.

5 There are two ways to finish this dish: either remove the ribs and cook them on the barbecue, or remove the lid from the dish and cook in the oven at 425°F/220°C/Gas 7 for 10 minutes. Keep the sauce to serve with the ribs.

TO MAKE THE SLAW

1 If you are making the mayonnaise, whisk together the egg yolks, mustard, and salt in a bowl. Then very gradually add the oil, stirring constantly and vigorously so that it emulsifies. Continue to add all—or most of—the oil. When safely mixed together, add the vinegar and beer. Keep in a jar in the refrigerator and it'll last for a few weeks.

2 To make the slaw, take a large bowl and combine 3 tablespoons of mayo with the crème fraîche, orange juice, cider vinegar, and seasoning. Add all the vegetables and mix well. Place in the refrigerator until ready.

EAT IT WITH...

I once spent a very drunk evening drinking IPA and Bourbon, where we tried to select a Bourbon to go with each of the beers as we drank them. That's part of the inspiration for this match and the actual dish itself. The IPA is great with the ribs and sweet-smoky sauce, while the Bourbon gives an extra kick to the combo.

PILSNER MEATLOAF

1 onion, finely chopped
1 tablespoon butter, plus extra for
greasing
2 garlic cloves, finely chopped
2 bay leaves
1 teaspoon dried marjoram
½ teaspoon ground cumin
1⅔ cup (100g) fresh breadcrumbs
½ cup (100ml) Pilsner
1¾lb (800g) ground (minced) meat
(I use 18oz/500g pork and
10½oz/300g beef, where plenty
of fat is good)
1 teaspoon each sea salt, black
pepper, and white pepper
(plus extra for seasoning)
2 egg yolks, beaten
2 tablespoons Dijon mustard

There's an awesome butcher's shop in Prague called Naše Maso. The meat is magnificent and they also cook some of their products in the small shop, including sausages, a glorious burger, and the best meatloaf I've ever had. They don't use beer in their recipe, but I've adapted a version to include Pilsner Urquell, the classic Czech brew.

1 Preheat the oven to 350°F/180°C/Gas 4 and grease a deep square baking dish with some butter.

2 Fry the onion slowly in the butter until soft, then add the garlic, bay leaves, marjoram, and cumin, season with sea salt and black pepper, and cook for a few minutes. Remove from the heat and leave to cool.

3 Place the breadcrumbs in a bowl and pour over the beer so it soaks into the crumbs.

4 Combine the ground (minced) meat with the sea salt and peppers in another larger bowl, then add the soaked breadcrumbs and onions.

5 Use your hands to mix everything together and then pour in the egg yolks. Mix again until everything is evenly combined.

6 Press the meat mixture into the baking dish and bake in the oven for 45 minutes. After 20 minutes, glaze the top of the meatloaf with the Dijon mustard, then return to the oven. (If there's a lot of liquid in the dish, then drain this off when you add the mustard glaze.)

7 Remove from the oven and allow to cool for 15–20 minutes before serving.

8 Serve simply with some fresh bread and mustard for a snack or cook some mashed potato and steamed vegetables for a main meal.

EAT IT WITH...

A classic Pilsner Urquell or other great Czech lager is the best, with other choices including Kozel, Budvar, and Bernard. It's got the bitter-sweet balance of malt and hops which is ideal with the meat fat and herbs in the dish.

EAT IT WITH...

A glass of Tripel is undoubtedly the best choice here, especially the one you cooked with, but, given the flavor combinations, a nice alternative would be an IPA. Something smooth, a little sweet, and with a big citrusy aroma—this will work well with the garlic, thyme, and ground coriander used in the different dishes.

TRIPLE TRIPEL PORK

SERVES 4

FOR THE TRIPEL-BRINED PORK

3 tablespoons sugar

3 tablespoons salt

4 garlic cloves, roughly chopped

1 white onion, roughly chopped

12 coriander seeds

12 black peppercorns

¼ of a fresh lemon

Small bunch of fresh thyme

8 pork chops (chicken thighs also work)

1 bottle of Tripel, reserving ¼ cup (50ml)

FOR THE TRIPEL BOULANGÈRE POTATOES

2¼lb (1kg) potatoes, peeled and thinly sliced

2 onions, thinly sliced

2 garlic cloves, finely chopped

1 tablespoon fresh thyme leaves

¾ cup (200ml) hot chicken stock

1 tablespoon Tripel

1 cup (100g) grated cheese (such as Gruyère or Parmesan)

4 tablespoons (50g) butter, cubed

Salt and black pepper

FOR THE TRIPEL AND HONEY CARROTS

18oz (500g) Chantenay or small carrots

4 tablespoons (50g) butter

2 tablespoons honey

1 tablespoon Tripel

1 whole garlic clove

2 slices of fresh lemon

½ teaspoon ground coriander

Salt and black pepper

I love Tripels and wanted to create a whole meal using one bottle of great beer, so this is a Tripel-brined pork chop, Tripel-spiked Boulangère potatoes, and Tripel and honey carrots. I used Westmalle, but any good Tripel is fine and will add the depth of alcohol that you expect from a strong beer, plus a little fruity, peppery flavor in the background—it's a powerful beer, which is why only a small amount is needed in two of the recipes below.

TRIPEL-BRINED PORK

1 Begin the day before—or at least the morning before—by brining the pork. Mix all of the ingredients together in a large, lidded plastic container, ensuring the sugar and salt are dissolved, and then add the pork chops. Top up with just enough water to cover. Put the lid on the container and refrigerate for 8–24 hours.

2 Remove the container from the refrigerator an hour or so before you're ready to cook the pork. Use some paper towels to dry off the excess liquid from each chop and then broil (grill) or griddle for 5–10 minutes on each side.

TRIPEL BOULANGÈRE POTATOES

1 Preheat the oven to 350°F/180°C/Gas 4.

2 Layer the potatoes, onion, garlic, and thyme in a large baking dish, season with salt and black pepper, and continue layering in this way until you've used up all the ingredients.

3 Pour over the stock and beer, and then top with the cheese and butter. Bake for 1 hour, or until the potatoes are soft.

TRIPEL AND HONEY CARROTS

1 Tear off a large piece of aluminum foil and fold it in half. Fold up the edges of the foil to create a makeshift baking dish. Place all the ingredients in the foil, season with salt and black pepper, and then wrap the foil to seal. Bake in the same oven as the potatoes for 45 minutes, opening up the foil for the final 15 minutes.

VIETNAMESE SAISON PORK
WITH NOODLES AND SAISON NUOC CHAM

I went to Vietnam while writing my third book, *The Best Beer in the World*, and I've been obsessed with cooking Vietnamese food ever since. This recipe adds zesty, spicy Saison to one of my favorite dishes, *bun thit*, which is served over rice noodles with salad, fragrant herbs, and *nuoc cham*, the ever-present Vietnamese dipping sauce, to which I've added more beer. My one tip is that the more caramelized you get the pork, the better.

SERVES 4

FOR THE VIETNAMESE SAISON PORK

14–18oz (400–500g) pork neck fillet
4 tablespoons fish sauce
2 tablespoons soy sauce
4 tablespoons Saison
2 tablespoons sugar
1 tablespoon honey
2 lemon grass stalks, outer layer
    removed and very finely chopped
2 garlic cloves, very finely chopped
1in (2.5cm) piece of ginger, peeled
    and very finely chopped
2 shallots (or 3 scallions/spring
    onions), very finely chopped
Black pepper

FOR THE SAISON NUOC CHAM

2 tablespoons water
2 tablespoons beer
2 tablespoons fish sauce
2 tablespoons lime juice
1 tablespoon sugar
Optional extras: ½ chili and ½ garlic
    clove, both very finely chopped

TO SERVE: cooked rice noodles,
    carrot strips, fresh cilantro
    (coriander), Thai basil or mint
    leaves, crushed peanuts, and
    chopped scallions (spring onions)

1   To make the Saison pork, cut the neck fillet into small cubes and set to one side in a large bowl.

2   Mix the fish sauce, soy sauce, Saison, sugar, and honey in a bowl. Season with some black pepper and then add the chopped lemon grass, garlic, ginger, and shallots. Pour the mixture over the pork, ensuring that the meat is completely covered, and leave in the refrigerator for at least 2 hours (or up to 8 hours).

3   To cook, either grill the pork on a barbecue until it takes on a nice caramelized char, or in a roasting pan in a hot oven at 425°F/220°C/Gas 7 for 30 minutes.

4   To make the Saison Nuoc Cham, simply combine all of the ingredients in a bowl, adding chili to taste.

5   To serve, place some cooked rice noodles in a bowl. Place the pork on top, along with the carrots, lots of fresh herbs, crushed peanuts, and scallions (spring onions) and then drizzle a few tablespoons of the Saison Nuoc Cham over the whole dish.

BEER STYLE:
SAISON

EAT IT WITH...

Saison is a great choice, as the dry, herbal quality really zings with all the spicy ingredients, plus it loves the balance between sweet, salty, and sour. Fantôme Saison, Ommegang Hennepin, and Brew By Numbers Saison are all excellent choices.

SERVES 4

SPICY WITBIER
FISH BURGERS
WITH SRIRACHA-WIT SLAW

The fruity-spicy flavors in Witbier make it a great match for Southeast Asian food. Used in these fish burgers, the beer adds its own fragrant depth that works alongside the other ingredients. The beer also goes into a slaw that uses crème fraîche instead of mayonnaise to make it lighter. You can eat these burgers on their own, add some roasted sweet potatoes on the side, or pop them in a bun.

FOR THE WITBIER FISH BURGERS

2 garlic cloves
A small thumb-sized piece of fresh ginger or galangal, peeled
1–2 chili peppers
2 lemon grass stalks, outer layer removed
2 scallions (spring onions)
Handful of fresh cilantro (coriander)
2 tablespoons Witbier
2 tablespoons fish sauce
Zest of 1 lime (reserve the juice for the slaw)
½ teaspoon ground coriander
½ teaspoon ground turmeric
1 tablespoon sugar or honey
18oz (500g) fish (a mix of salmon and white fish is good), skins and bones removed
Olive or sesame oil, for cooking

FOR THE SRIRACHA-WIT SLAW

2 tablespoons crème fraîche
2 tablespoons Witbier
1 tablespoon Sriracha (or other hot sauce)
Juice of ½ lime
1 carrot, grated and the juice squeezed out
4 scallions (spring onions), chopped
½ white cabbage, finely chopped
¾ cup (100g) edamame beans (optional but good)
Salt and black pepper
Handful of fresh cilantro (coriander)
1 teaspoon toasted sesame seeds

1. To make the fish burgers, roughly chop the garlic, ginger/galangal, chili peppers, lemon grass, scallions (spring onions), and cilantro (coriander). Place with all the remaining ingredients (apart from the fish) in a blender and blitz for 3–5 minutes until you have a smooth paste.

2. Add the fish to the food-processor, and blitz for a few more minutes until you have a thick burger mixture.

3. Wet your fingers and then divide the burger mixture into patties–you can make four large ones or 6–8 smaller ones.

4. Heat some olive or sesame oil in a large, heavy-based saucepan or griddle and cook the burgers for around 5 minutes on each side, depending on how fat they are.

5. To make the slaw, mix all the wet ingredients together in a large bowl. Add the chopped vegetables and edamame beans (if using), stir to combine, and check the seasoning.

6. To serve, sprinkle with the fresh cilantro (coriander) and toasted sesame seeds.

FOR THE SAISON SALMON

4 garlic cloves

1oz (25g) fresh dill, plus extra to serve

⅓ cup (100ml) Saison

2 bay leaves

1 teaspoon toasted and crushed
  coriander seeds (ground coriander
  just isn't the same here)

1 tablespoon honey

4 salmon fillets

2 lemons (1 juiced and the other cut
  into thick slices)

Salt and black pepper

Flatbreads, to serve

FOR THE BEET AND DILL
SALAD

5½oz (150g) cream cheese (or
  creamed goats' cheese)

1oz (25g) fresh dill, plus extra to
  serve

Juice of ½ lemon

3 tablespoons Saison

1 tablespoon extra virgin olive oil

½ teaspoon ground coriander
  (ideally freshly ground from
  toasted seeds)

18oz (500g) cooked beets (beetroot),
  chopped into ½in (1cm) cubes

Salt and white pepper

1oz (25g) toasted hazelnuts, roughly
  crushed, to serve

SAISON SALMON
WITH BEET AND DILL SALAD

This is all about the beet (beetroot) salad. Sure, the Saison Salmon is really nice, but it's the beets that are the star. It's inspired by a dish I had in an East London restaurant that specializes in grilled meats and Middle Eastern side dishes. The dill has an amazing, savory, aniseedy quality, while the hazelnuts give a toasty crunch. With Saison as one of the ingredients, and also poured on the side, it lifts the dish majestically. The salad also works really well with the Kriek Lamb on page 86.

1 To make the Saison salmon, preheat the oven to 400°F/200°C/Gas 6.

2 Combine all the ingredients, apart from the salmon and lemon slices, in a deep roasting pan.

3 Season the salmon fillet skins and place skin-side up in the roasting pan. Arrange the lemon slices around the fillets. Bake in the oven for 15 minutes. When cooked, drizzle some of the cooking liquid over the salmon before serving.

4 To make the beet (beetroot) and dill salad, mix all the ingredients in a bowl, apart from the beets and hazelnuts. When combined, add the beets and stir into the sauce. Season with salt and pepper, according to taste.

5 Enjoy the salmon with the salad, sprinkling over more fresh dill and the toasted hazelnuts when you serve. Fresh flatbreads work well on the side—simply follow the recipe for lager chapatis on page 94, but use some Saison in these and sprinkle with ground coriander.

EAT IT WITH...

Saison Dupont is the first beer I had with this salad and I've yet to find a better pairing. There's something in how the earthy, orangey, spicy flavors in the beer work with the beets, dill, and cheese and enhance everything. It's one of my top beer matches and one of my top beer side dishes.

BELGIAN BEEF BRISKET

This is my evolution of the classic Belgian Carbonnade, which is the kind of dish that's been around for years and sits alongside meat and ale pies as one of the best-known beer recipes. By using brisket, and giving it a long, slow cook with loads of onions and an apple (I cook it into the sauce rather than serving apple on the side, which you see in Belgium), you get this meltingly tender meat that sucks up all of the toasty, fruity flavors of the dark Belgian ale. The beer to use is a Belgian dark ale such as Chimay Blue, St Bernardus 8, or La Trappe Quadrupel. This is classically served with fries, which is great, but you could also serve it inside brioche buns like a Belgian kind of Sloppy Joe (let's call it a Sloppy Jos).

SERVES 4-6

2¼lb (1kg) beef brisket
1 tablespoon each butter and olive oil
4 large onions, quartered
3 garlic cloves, crushed
½ teaspoon each ground cinnamon and ground coriander
1 teaspoon fresh thyme leaves
2 bay leaves
2 cups (500ml) hot beef stock
2 cups (500ml) dark Belgian beer
2 tablespoons brown sugar
1 apple, peeled, cored, and grated
1 tablespoon Dijon mustard
Sea salt and black pepper

1 Preheat the oven to 325°F/160°C/Gas 3. Season the brisket well with sea salt and black pepper.

2 Brown the brisket all over in the butter and oil in a large flameproof casserole dish on the stovetop. Set the meat to one side.

3 Add the onions to the dish and cook for a few minutes until they begin to caramelize, then add the garlic, cinnamon, coriander, thyme, and bay leaves.

4 Add the stock, then the beer (reserving around ¼ cup/50ml of the beer), sugar, apple, and mustard, and return the brisket to the dish.

5 Bring everything to a simmer, put the lid on the dish, and cook in the oven for 4–5 hours, checking every hour or so. You want the sauce to be thick and reduced, but not boiled away.

6 Before serving, pour the remaining ¼ cup (50ml) of beer into the sauce.

BEER STYLE:
BELGIAN DUBBEL

EAT IT WITH...

The dryness in a Belgian Dubbel makes it a refreshing match for this hearty dish, where the dried fruit flavors in the beer are also able to enhance the meat's depth. Try Ommegang Abbey Ale, Boulevard The Sixth Glass, Holgate Double Trouble, or a classic Belgian like Maredsous or St Bernardus.

BLACK LAGER YAKIUDON

I'm sure I'm not alone in my first experience of cooking with beer being the kind where you happen to be drinking and making dinner at the same time, have a flash of inspiration, and decide to pour some beer into whatever's in the pan in front of you. For me, it was into risottos at university, then into things like chilis and pasta sauces, then into just about anything else that was on the stovetop. I still like to cook that way today and enjoy quick recipes where I can open a beer and drink while cooking, also adding some to the dish, as with these noodles (where measuring the beer can be done in splashes rather than tablespoons if you wish, with one splash being roughly equivalent to one tablespoon). Asahi Black is the beer I use here.

SERVES 2

6 tablespoons soy sauce
6 tablespoons Black Lager
1 tablespoon superfine (caster) sugar
1 tablespoon mirin or sake (optional)
7oz (200g) beef steak (or tofu, if you prefer), finely sliced
10½oz (300g) udon noodles
1 tablespoon sesame oil
Small bunch of scallions (spring onions), chopped
1 garlic clove
Handful of beansprouts
1 bok choi (pak choi), chopped
1 carrot, finely chopped
4–6 chestnut mushrooms, sliced

1 Mix half the soy sauce and beer (so 3 tablespoons of each) with the sugar and mirin or sake, stirring in a bowl until the sugar dissolves. Add the sliced beef or tofu and marinate for up to 1 hour.

2 Cook the udon noodles according to the instructions on the packet and set to one side (pre-cooked noodles are fine for this dish).

3 Heat the sesame oil in a large wok. When the oil is hot, add the beef or tofu (leaving behind any excess marinade) and stir-fry for 1 minute.

4 Add the scallions (spring onions) and garlic, cook for a further minute, then add the beansprouts and other vegetables. Stir-fry for a couple of minutes, then add the cooked noodles and the remaining soy sauce and beer. Cook for 2 more minutes to heat the noodles through before serving.

BEER STYLE:
BLACK LAGER

EAT IT WITH...

The caramel and cocoa sweetness in an Asian Black Lager, such as Asahi, as well as it's dry and refreshing finish, make this the best match here. It's light, yet full of flavor; it shares similar flavors with the soy sauce and the sweeter ingredients; plus, it's an unchallenged and very satisfyingly simple pairing. Other Black Lagers to look for include Rogue Dirtoir and Kozel Dark.

18oz (500g) pork belly, chopped into 1in (2cm) cubes

⅓ cup (100ml) water

⅓ cup (100ml) soy sauce

2 tablespoons sugar

2 tablespoons honey

4 whole star anise

1 teaspoon five spice

½ teaspoon dried chili flakes

4 garlic cloves

11–12fl oz (330–350ml) Dunkel Weizen

Cooked white rice and steamed broccoli or bok choi (pak choi)

DUNKEL WEIZEN AND STAR ANISE PORK BELLY

You won't believe how good this will make your kitchen smell until you've cooked it. As the pork slowly softens, the sauce gets thicker and richer and sweeter, perfumed with the wonderful scent of honey and star anise (I love star anise and five spice—it has a beer-friendly sweet fragrance). The result is astonishing—especially considering the minimal (and cheap) ingredients used—and gives a sticky, sweet, rich bowl of pork that's best served on a bowl of white rice. The Dunkel Weizen, a dark wheat beer, gives some of its own sweet spiciness, although if you can't find one to use, then go for a Black Lager.

1 Preheat the oven to 300°F/150°C/Gas 2.

2 Boil some water in a large saucepan and then drop in the pork cubes for 30 seconds. Drain the pork.

3 Heat a large flameproof casserole dish on the stovetop. Brown the pork on all sides (you might need to do this in a couple of batches). You shouldn't need any cooking fat for this because the fat from the pork should render out (in fact, you may wish to drain some of this off before you continue cooking).

4 Return all the pork to the hot casserole dish, add the water, and allow to bubble for 1 minute.

5 Add the soy sauce, followed by all the other ingredients, saving the beer till last (and reserving around ¼ cup/50ml).

6 Bring to a simmer, put the lid on the dish, and cook in the oven for 1½–2 hours. Check after an hour and then every 15 minutes from there—the pork is ready when the sauce is very thick, sticky, and almost completely reduced.

7 Pour in the remaining beer before serving to give the dish a lift. Serve with some white rice and steamed broccoli or bok choi (pak choi).

EAT IT WITH...

It's a powerful dish that a Dark Wheat Beer or Dark Lager can stand up to, adding a refreshing quality to the richness in the pork. Dark Wheat is ideal as it adds some extra peppery and spicy flavors. Erdinger and Weihenstephaner both have readily available (and tasty) versions.

BEER STYLE: PALE ALE

EAT IT WITH...

A Pale Ale is a great choice here, loving the citrus and the avocado, where something especially juicy or lime-like is ideal. Try The Kernel Citra Pale Ale, Three Floyds Zombie Dust, or Little Creatures Pale Ale.

LAGER AND LIME CHICKEN TACOS
WITH AVOCADO AND LAGER SALSA

Lager and lime is a curious British combination that is quite literal: it's just a pint of lager with a dash of lime cordial. This takes that concept and turns it into a Mexican-inspired dish of lager-and-lime-brined chicken, topped with salsa, and wrapped in beer tacos–the recipe for these is great for either small tacos or larger tortillas. This is also a great recipe for using up any unwanted lager you might happen to have in the refrigerator.

SERVES 4

FOR THE LAGER AND LIME CHICKEN

14oz (400g) chicken thighs, skinned, boned, and diced
1 bottle of lager
1¼ cups (300ml) water
Juice of 3 limes
3 tablespoons sugar
3 tablespoons salt
12 coriander seeds
12 black peppercorns
4 garlic cloves, roughly chopped
4 chili peppers, roughly chopped
Plus, to cook: Salt, black pepper, some cayenne pepper (optional), and 1 whole lime (halved)

FOR THE LAGER TACOS

Heaping 2 cups (250g) masa harina flour
Pinch of salt
Scant 1½ cups (330ml) lager

FOR THE SALSA

2 ripe avocados, peeled and stoned
⅔ cup (100g) canned corn (sweetcorn)
2 tablespoons lager
2 teaspoons salt
Juice of ½ lime
1 green chili pepper, finely diced

TO SERVE: ¼ cup (50g) goats' cheese and some fresh cilantro (coriander)

TO MAKE THE LAGER AND LIME CHICKEN

1 In a large, sealable plastic container, mix the lager, water, and lime juice to make a brine. Add the sugar and salt, stirring until everything is combined, and then add the rest of the ingredients. Place the chicken in the brine, put the lid on the container, and keep in the refrigerator for up to 24 hours.

2 Preheat the oven to 425°F/220°C/Gas 7. Remove the thighs from the brine and pat them dry with some paper towel. Add extra seasoning and some cayenne pepper if you like your tacos hot. Place the thighs on a baking tray, along with the lime halves so that they caramelize, and cook for approximately 30 minutes. You can also cook the chicken thighs on a barbecue.

TO MAKE THE TACOS

1 Mix the masa harina flour and salt in a bowl. Add the lager and mix into a smooth dough with a clay-like consistency. Leave to rest for 15 minutes and knead again.

2 Divide the dough into small balls (you should get 10–12). Flatten the balls of dough until they are about ⅛in (3mm) thick. A rolling pin works fine for this unless you have a tortilla press. Either way, place the dough balls between two pieces of plastic wrap (clingfilm) when flattening them.

3 Cook the tacos in a dry frying pan over a medium-high heat for about 30 seconds on each side. Place in a warm oven until needed.

TO MAKE THE SALSA

1 Chop the avocado into ½in (1cm) cubes. In a small bowl, mix the avocado with the corn kernels (sweetcorn), lager, salt, lime, and chili pepper, and place in the refrigerator until ready. To serve, place a chicken thigh in a soft taco, top with some avocado salsa, and add some goats' cheese and a few leaves of fresh cilantro (coriander).

FOR THE BEER MEATBALLS

2oz (50g) crackers or breadcrumbs
⅓ cup (100ml) beer
18oz (500g) ground (minced) meat
(beef, pork, or a combination
of both)
1 egg, beaten
1 teaspoon Dijon mustard
1 teaspoon onion powder
⅓ cup (30g) grated Parmesan cheese
Olive oil, for frying
Salt and black pepper

FOR THE BEER TOMATO SAUCE

1 onion, finely chopped
Olive oil, for frying
2 garlic cloves, finely chopped
2 x 14oz (400g) cans chopped
tomatoes
¾ cup (200ml) beer
1 tablespoon sugar
1 tablespoon balsamic vinegar
½ teaspoon dried chili flakes
(optional but good)
A few freshly torn basil leaves
Salt and black pepper

TO SERVE: Cooked spaghetti for
4 people

BEER STYLE:
STOUT

EAT IT WITH...
The beer you used in the recipe is
ideal and Stout is a good choice,
though a dark Belgian beer also
works very well.

BEER MEATBALLS
AND TOMATO SAUCE WITH SPAGHETTI

Spaghetti and meatballs are even better when you add
beer. I've made this dish with Belgian Blonde and Stout.
The Blonde gave it a sweeter, fruitier flavor, which was
really nice, while the Stout gave a greater richness. Both
work, so go with your favorite brew—just make sure you use
the same beer in the meatballs and the sauce.

1 To make the tomato sauce, soften the onion in a little olive oil
in a large saucepan. Add the garlic and tomatoes, then the beer,
sugar, balsamic vinegar, and chili flakes (if using). Simmer for
around 20 minutes until the sauce gradually reduces.

2 To make the meatballs, crush the crackers or breadcrumbs into
a fine crumb and place in a small bowl. Pour in the beer and
allow to soak until the liquid is absorbed.

3 In a large bowl, combine the ground (minced) meat with the
egg, mustard, onion powder, and Parmesan cheese, and season
with salt and black pepper.

4 Add the beer-soaked crackers or breadcrumbs to the meat.
Mix together (your hands work best for this) until everything
is well combined.

5 Take small amounts of the meat mixture and shape them into
golf-ball-sized meatballs. Set the meatballs to one side.

6 Heat a tablespoon of olive oil in a large saucepan. Add the
meatballs and brown them on the outside, moving them
around regularly to prevent them sticking and burning. After
around 10 minutes, pour the tomato sauce over the meatballs
and simmer for 10–15 minutes. Check the seasoning and add
the fresh basil leaves.

7 To serve, pour the meatballs and tomato sauce over plates
of spaghetti.

BEER BOLOGNESE

Everyone has a recipe for spaghetti bolognese, right? It's just like chili in that everyone has their own version and does it their own way, even though it's all based on the same dish. Personally, I think alcohol is essential—whether this is wine or beer—and so is a long, slow cook. There are a few beer options: a Belgian Dubbel gives a sweetly spicy flavor, a Smoked Porter gives more of a meaty oomph, and a Bock gives a great background malt depth, so the choice is yours.

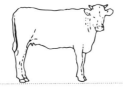

SERVES 4-6

18oz (500g) ground (minced) meat (beef, pork, or a combination of both)
2 tablespoons (25g) butter, for frying
4 rashers streaky bacon or pancetta, chopped
1 large onion, finely chopped
1 teaspoon sugar
3 garlic cloves, roughly chopped
6–8 chestnut mushrooms, finely chopped
2 carrots, finely diced
14oz (400g) can plum tomatoes
1 bottle beer (Smoked Porter, Dubbel, or Bock)
2 bay leaves
Salt and black pepper (go big on the pepper)

1 Preheat the oven to 325°F/160°C/Gas 3.

2 In a large cast-iron casserole dish, brown the ground (minced) meat in the butter for a few minutes and then remove from the pan.

3 Add the bacon or pancetta and fry for 1 minute before adding the onion and sugar, allowing them to soften. Add the garlic, mushrooms, and carrots, and stir for a few more minutes. Then return the meat to the dish.

4 Pour in the tomatoes and beer, and bring to a gentle simmer. Add the bay leaves and season with salt and black pepper. Put a lid on the dish and cook in the oven for 2 hours, stirring after 1 hour and then checking that the bolognese is not too dry as the 2-hour point approaches—add some hot beef stock, more beer, or water if necessary.

5 Serve with spaghetti or another pasta of your choice.

BEER STYLE:
DUBBEL

EAT IT WITH...
A Belgian Dubbel is a great choice, especially Rochefort 6 or 8. If you used a Smoked Porter, then go for a smoked beer such as Schlenkerla Rauchbier or Alaskan Smoked Porter.

PORK CHEEKS IN CIDER

Cider is great in the kitchen, especially if you've got something strong and dry. Also, unlike beer, it isn't bitter and so is kind in the cooking process. This is one of those slow-cooked recipes that comes out steaming, warming, and soft enough to eat with a spoon, with the apples in the cider giving a great background flavor to the pork.

SERVES 4

8 pig cheeks
2 tablespoons olive oil
1 onion, finely chopped
1 stick celery, finely chopped
1 large carrot, finely chopped
2 garlic cloves, finely chopped
3½oz (100g) smoked bacon or
  pancetta
1 tablespoon tomato paste (purée)
1 cooking apple, peeled and grated
2 cups (500ml) dry cider
2 cups (500ml) hot chicken stock
2 bay leaves
6 fresh sage leaves, chopped
2 rosemary sprigs
Dash of Worcestershire sauce
Salt and black pepper

1 Preheat the oven to 300°F/150°C/Gas 2.

2 Season the pig cheeks with salt and black pepper, and then brown in the olive oil in a large flameproof casserole dish. Remove the cheeks from the dish and set to one side.

3 Soften the onion, celery, and carrot in the same dish over a medium heat for a couple of minutes.

4 Add the garlic and bacon (or pancetta), followed by the tomato paste (purée) and grated apple. Cook through for 3–4 minutes. Return the cheeks to the dish and add the remaining ingredients.

5 Bring to a simmer, put the lid on the dish, and place in the oven for 2½ hours, stirring occasionally. (Leave the dish uncovered for the final 15 minutes if you would prefer a thicker sauce).

6 Serve with mustard-mashed potato and some green vegetables.

EAT IT WITH...

A classic Somerset Scrumpy or an American hard cider–just make sure that it's not too sweet or fizzy; you want the cider to be refreshing, dry, and a little bit tart.

BEER PASTA

Putting beer in pasta dough is a neat twist on a classic recipe, where a smooth, slightly sweet Porter or Stout is a great choice–I like to use Anchor's Porter or Sam Smith's Oatmeal Stout. And, while you can serve this with any pasta sauce you like, my preference is to keep it super simple and either make a classic carbonara, cacio e pepe, or anchovy, garlic, chili, and lemon.

SERVES 6

18oz (500g) Tipo "00" flour, plus extra for dusting

1 teaspoon sea salt

6 egg yolks, beaten

1 tablespoon olive oil

¾ cup (200ml) Porter, at room temperature

BEER STYLE: PORTER

EAT IT WITH...

A smooth, easy-drinking Porter or Stout with low roast, bitterness, and acidity are best. Anchor Porter is ideal, plus it's excellent with the cheese and pepper. If you're serving cacio e pepe, then a dry-hopped Saison is great–the fruity hops are excellent with the cheese, while the pepper and yeast share some qualities–Saison Dupont have a good one.

1 Place the flour and salt in a bowl and make a well in the center. Add the egg yolks, olive oil, and some of the beer to the well, then use a fork to mix the wet and dry ingredients together, gradually adding more beer and mixing until you can pick up the dough and knead it.

2 Knead the dough on a flour-dusted surface for around 10 minutes. Get pretty aggressive here. Pull, push, punch, fold, roll, whatever, just get it all nicely kneaded together until you have a smooth dough (adding more flour or beer at any time if it's too wet or dry). Roll the dough into a ball, cover with plastic wrap (clingfilm), and place in the refrigerator for 30–60 minutes.

3 A pasta machine is the easiest thing to use at this stage, but you can use a rolling pin instead. Either way it's best to divide the dough into smaller balls (between golf- and tennis-ball-sized).

4 If you have a pasta machine, roll out the dough until it's long and thin–you're aiming for tagliatelle here. If you're using a rolling pin, then just persevere and keep on rolling that pin, stretching out the dough, folding it back on itself, then rolling it some more until you have a long, thin, flat piece of dough (dust some more flour over it if it gets sticky)–it's going to take some muscle to make this happen.

5 Roll the pasta dough lengthwise into a cigar shape and cut into thin rounds (less than ½in/1cm) thick), which you then unravel. Place the unraveled rounds of dough on a piece of damp paper towel so that they don't dry out. Repeat until you've used up all the dough. (If you wish, you can freeze the uncooked pasta in a freezer bag until needed–then cook directly from frozen.)

6 To cook, boil lots of water in a large saucepan. Add some salt and then cook the pasta–it should cook within a minute or two. Drain.

7 To serve, try a classic cacio e pepe recipe and mix the pasta with butter, lots of grated Parmesan cheese, and freshly cracked black pepper. Alternatively, cook some anchovies in a large frying pan in two tablespoons of their own oil, add a clove of finely chopped garlic, and some dried chili flakes, then stir in the pasta, and finish with a squeeze of lemon juice.

DUVEL AND ANCHOVY SAUCE

FOR PASTA

I love Duvel and, as there are always bottles in my refrigerator, I often cook with it. Duvel can add a great depth of alcohol richness to dishes, plus it has some gentler aromatic qualities that work well with lots of different ingredients, especially garlic, Parmesan cheese, salt, and black pepper. This sauce is ideal as a quick supper, using mostly storecupboard staples. It also works well on top of pork or chicken.

SERVES 2

Pasta of choice (such as spaghetti),
   for 2 people
6–8 anchovies (from a jar or can)
1 garlic clove, finely chopped
1¼ cups (300ml) crème fraîche
¼ cup (50ml) Duvel or Tripel
1oz (25g) grated Parmesan cheese,
   plus extra for serving
Handful of freshly torn basil leaves
Juice of ½ lemon
Black pepper

1 First, cook the pasta you're serving with the sauce. Gnocchi is also good.

2 Meanwhile, gently fry the anchovies in some of their own oil in a saucepan until they begin to melt with the heat. Add the garlic and cook for a few more minutes.

3 Add the crème fraîche and stir through well. As the sauce comes to a simmer, add the beer and Parmesan cheese, and heat through for a couple of minutes.

4 Add the basil and lemon juice, and season with lots of black pepper. Remove the pan from the heat and mix into the cooked pasta (or gnocchi).

5 Serve with extra grated Parmesan and black pepper, as desired.

BEER STYLE:
BELGIAN GOLDEN ALE OR TRIPEL

EAT IT WITH...
A bottle of Duvel or a Belgian Tripel, like Westmalle, is a good choice. Alternatives would be a Saison or Witbier–all of which could also be used in the recipe.

BEER CHICKEN PARMA

I went to Melbourne and asked some mates what food I should eat and a Chicken Parma is what they all said. It's proper Aussie pub food: a breaded chicken breast topped with tomato sauce, a thick slice of ham, and melted cheese. This is the beerier version of that and you should use a nice fruity Golden or Summer Ale in all aspects of this.

SERVES 2

FOR THE BREADED CHICKEN

2 chicken breasts
1 bottle of beer
3 tablespoons sugar
3 tablespoons salt
3 garlic cloves, roughly chopped
10 fresh basil leaves
4 tablespoons fresh breadcrumbs
1 tablespoon grated Parmesan cheese
2 tablespoons all-purpose (plain) flour
1 egg, beaten
2 thick slices of ham
Salt and black pepper

FOR THE TOMATO SAUCE

14oz (400g) can chopped tomatoes
1 teaspoon sugar
Salt and black pepper

FOR THE BEER CHEESE SAUCE

Follow the recipe for The Ultimate Beer Cheese Sauce on page 104, but use the same quantities as for the Croque Monsieur and include plenty of Parmesan cheese in the mix.

1 Make a brine for the chicken by mixing the beer with the sugar, salt, garlic, and basil in a plastic container with a lid. Place the chicken in the brine, top up with water, and keep refrigerated for 8–24 hours.

2 Preheat the oven to 350°F/180°C/Gas 4. Remove the chicken from the brine and dry off any excess liquid with some paper towel. Place the chicken between two sheets of plastic wrap (clingfilm) and bash with a mallet or frying pan to flatten. Discard the plastic wrap.

3 Mix the breadcrumbs and Parmesan cheese in a bowl, and season with some salt and black pepper. Place the flour and beaten egg in two separate bowls. Take each chicken breast and dip it in the flour, egg, and then the breadcrumbs. Place the chicken on a baking tray and cook in the oven for around 20 minutes.

4 To make the tomato sauce, place all of the ingredients in a saucepan and cook over a medium heat until the sauce has reduced. Keep warm until needed.

5 To make the beer cheese sauce, follow the instructions for the Croque Monsieur on page 105 and make sure the sauce is nice and thick.

6 When the chicken is cooked, remove from the oven and turn on the broiler (grill). Place a teaspoon or two of tomato sauce on the chicken, followed by a slice of ham, and then a few spoons of the beer-cheese sauce. Place under the broiler (grill) until the topping bubbles.

7 Serve the chicken with fries and a side salad.

EAT IT WITH...

I really like this dish with an Oatmeal or Milk Stout. It likes the sharper and fruitier flavors in the dressing, plus it's great with the sweet-tart flavor of the lamb. A good alternative is a fruited wheat beer such as Founder's Rübæus or Kasteel Rouge.

KRIEK LAMB

WITH POMEGRANATE, PISTACHIO, AND GOATS' CHEESE SALAD

FOR THE KRIEK LAMB

1 cup (250ml) Kriek
3 tablespoons sugar
3 tablespoons salt
12 coriander seeds
1 teaspoon ground sumac
½ teaspoon ground cinnamon
  (or 1 cinnamon stick)
2 bay leaves
3 garlic cloves, roughly chopped
8–12 lamb cutlets (or 4 lamb
  leg steaks)

FOR THE POMEGRANATE, PISTACHIO, AND GOATS' CHEESE SALAD

Scant ½ cup (75g) rice, couscous, or
  quinoa, per person
Seeds of 1 pomegranate (reserve any
  spare juice)
¾ cup (100g) toasted pistachio nuts
  (shells removed)
5oz (150g) goats' cheese, cubed
Handful of fresh mint, finely
  chopped

FOR THE SALAD DRESSING

4 tablespoons Kriek
2 tablespoons lemon juice
2 tablespoons pomegranate juice
  (if possible)
4 tablespoons olive oil
1 tablespoon honey
½ teaspoon salt
½ teaspoon ground sumac

I love cooking this vibrant, fragrant dish with a Middle Eastern accent. Most of the beer is used as a brine, but some is reserved to make a salad dressing, giving a great acidity to the meal. Try not to leave out the sumac–it adds an integral tangy flavor to the recipe.

1 Create a brine for the lamb in a large plastic container with a lid by mixing the beer (reserving what is left in the bottle) with all of the ingredients (apart from the lamb). Stir well to dissolve the salt and sugar.

2 Place the lamb in the container and top up with water until it's covered with liquid. Cover and refrigerate for 8–24 hours.

3 When you're ready to cook, remove the lamb from the brine, dry off any excess liquid with some paper towels, and broil (grill) or griddle for a few minutes on each side. Allow to rest for 5 minutes before serving.

4 To make the pomegranate, pistachio, and goats' cheese salad, prepare your choice of rice, couscous, or quinoa according to the instructions on the packet. Place the cooked grain in a large bowl and allow to cool for a few minutes. (If you're preparing the salad in advance, you can leave it to cool down completely and eat it cold.)

5 Spread the pomegranate seeds, pistachio nuts, goats' cheese, and mint over the salad grains.

6 To make the salad dressing, combine all of the ingredients and drizzle over the lamb and salad when serving.

RECIPE VARIATION:

A great vegetarian alternative is to slice an eggplant (aubergine) into the shape of fat fries and then grill or roast these with some olive oil and salt and black pepper (at 400°F/200°C/Gas 6 for around 25 minutes). While the eggplant is cooking, prepare the salad dressing, as described above. When the eggplant is cooked, soak it in the dressing for at least 10 minutes (or up to an hour). Serve at room temperature with the Pomegranate, Pistachio, and Goats' Cheese Salad.

TOAD IN THE HOLE
BEER ONION GRAVY AND STOUT MASH

This is a classic British dish that bakes sausages in a beer-batter pudding, with the beer lending a nice sweetness and malty depth. I like to use a Mild, Porter, or Stout for this recipe, but nothing too hop-bitter. The gravy is rich with more beer, while the potatoes are mashed with a small amount of Stout or dark beer, which adds a savory, roasted depth. It's traditional home-cooking with the addition of beer.

SERVES 4

FOR THE TOAD IN THE HOLE

1 cup (125g) plain flour
½ teaspoon salt
½ teaspoon white pepper
3 eggs, beaten
⅔ cup (150ml) milk
⅔ cup (150ml) Dark Beer
3–4 tablespoons olive oil
8 sausages
1 white onion, sliced

FOR THE BEER ONION GRAVY

2 red onions, sliced
2 tablespoons (25g) butter
3–4 fresh sage leaves, finely chopped
1 teaspoon sugar
1 teaspoon salt
1 tablespoon tomato paste (purée)
1 tablespoon all-purpose (plain) flour
¾ cup (200ml) hot beef stock
⅔ cup (150ml) Dark Beer

FOR THE STOUT MASH

2¼lb (1kg) potatoes, peeled and
   roughly chopped
6 tablespoons (75g) butter
¼ cup (50ml) Stout
Smoked salt and white pepper

TO MAKE THE TOAD IN THE HOLE

1. Prepare the batter for the toad in the hole in advance by combining the flour, salt, and pepper in a bowl.

2. Mix the beaten eggs with the milk and beer in a separate jug. Gradually pour the liquid into the dry ingredients, whisking until you have a smooth batter. Cover and place in the refrigerator until needed.

3. Preheat the oven to 425°F/220°C/Gas 7. Add a few tablespoons of the oil to a deep, wide baking dish and place in the middle of the oven. When the oil is hot, carefully remove the dish and arrange the sausages and onion over the bottom. Return to the oven for 10 minutes.

4. Remove the dish from the oven and gently pour the batter over the sausages and onion—be careful here, as the oil will be very hot and probably spit. Bake for a further 30 minutes.

TO MAKE THE GRAVY

1. Place the onion in a saucepan with the butter, sage leaves, sugar, and salt, and cook over a low heat until the onions are soft and sweet—this will take around 15 minutes.

2. Add the tomato paste (purée) and stir into the onion for a couple of minutes, before adding the flour and combining well.

3. Add the stock and stir to create a smooth, thick gravy. Pour in the beer and simmer for a couple of minutes.

TO MAKE THE STOUT MASH

1. While the toad in the hole and onion gravy are cooking, place the potatoes in a saucepan of cold, salted water. Bring to a boil and cook the potatoes for 15–20 minutes, or until they are soft.

2. Drain the potatoes and add the butter and Stout, season with the salt and pepper, and then mash until thick and smooth.

FOR THE SMOKED BEER PULLED PORK

To marinate: 1 teaspoon each sea salt, black pepper, brown sugar, superfine (caster) sugar, dried chili flakes, ground coriander, smoked paprika, onion powder, garlic powder, fennel seeds, and five spice

2¼lb (1kg) pork shoulder (ideally still boned)

2 tablespoons olive oil

2 large white onions, quartered

3 carrots, each chopped into 3–4 pieces

¾ cup (200ml) hot beef stock

2 cups (500ml) Smoked Beer

3 tablespoons malt or cider vinegar

4 garlic cloves

4 bay leaves

1 cinnamon stick

3 whole star anise

4 whole chili peppers (optional)

2 tablespoons brown sugar

FOR THE BEER ONIONS

1 red onion, halved and sliced into semicircles

1 fresh chili pepper (optional)

⅔ cup (150ml) Smoked Beer

⅔ cup (150ml) cider vinegar

½ cup (100g) sugar

1oz (25g) sea salt

FOR THE BEER TACOS

Follow the recipe for the Lager Tacos on page 77, but use either a Pale or a Dark Lager.

TO SERVE: Some smoked Cheddar cheese

SMOKED BEER PULLED PORK TACOS

WITH BEER ONIONS

I'm obsessed with tacos. This one takes pulled pork, cooks it in smoked beer, then tops it off with two further smoke-infused dishes: Smoked Beer Onions and smoked Cheddar cheese. For the smoked beer, you could use a Porter or Rauchbier.

TO MAKE THE PULLED PORK

1 Combine all the dry-rub marinade ingredients and rub them into the pork shoulder. Place in the refrigerator for 1–12 hours.

2 When ready to cook, preheat the oven to 300°F/150°C/Gas 2. Add the olive oil to a large lidded flameproof casserole dish, and brown the pork on all sides on the stovetop. Remove the pork from the dish and set to one side.

3 Brown the onion and carrots in the same dish for a few minutes, then add the stock, the beer, and the rest of the ingredients. Return the pork to the dish and bring to a simmer. Put the lid on the dish and cook in the oven for 3–4 hours, checking regularly toward the end of the cooking time to ensure the pork isn't boiling dry (add more water or beer if it does).

4 When cooked, remove the pork from the dish and place in a bowl. Use two forks to pull the meat apart. The remaining sauce can be reduced until thick, strained, and used in the tacos.

TO MAKE THE BEER ONIONS

1 Place the sliced onion in a jar or plastic container (you can add rings of fresh chilis if you wish), then pour in the smoked beer. Mix the cider vinegar with the sugar and sea salt in a saucepan. Boil for 5 minutes. Remove from the heat and pour over the onions. Allow to cool before serving.

TO SERVE: Take a warm taco and place some pulled pork on top, add some reduced cooking sauce (if you have any), the onions, and then some smoked cheese.

> **BEER STYLE:**
> # SMOKED PORTER
>
> ## EAT IT WITH...
> You might as well go all in on the smoke—use the beer you cooked with.

IPA AND CHEDDAR CHEESE BARLEY RISOTTO

The combination of IPA and strong Cheddar cheese is a marvelous thing. When added to this risotto, which ups the beer-ante by using pearl barley instead of risotto rice (although you can still use Arborio risotto rice if you prefer), the combination produces a hearty meal, in which the fruitiness of the beer is great with the cheese. Just choose a beer that's big on aroma, but low on bitterness.

SERVES 4

1 large white onion, finely chopped
1 large leek, finely chopped
1 tablespoon (15g) butter
1 tablespoon olive oil
2 garlic cloves, finely chopped
½ teaspoon finely chopped fresh thyme or rosemary leaves
1 teaspoon sugar
2 cups (400g) pearl barley (or Arborio risotto rice)
5¼ cups (1.2 liters) hot chicken or vegetable stock
¾ cup (200ml) IPA
1¼ cups (150g) grated strong Cheddar cheese
½ cup (50g) grated Parmesan cheese
Black pepper

1 Soften the onion and leek in the butter and olive oil in a saucepan for a few minutes.

2 Add the garlic, thyme/rosemary, and sugar, and season with black pepper. Stir for 2 minutes, before adding the pearl barley (or risotto rice) and stirring for a further minute.

3 Add a ladle of the stock, stirring until the grain has soaked up all the stock. Continue to add a ladle of stock at a time, stirring constantly—it helps to have a glass of beer in your other hand while cooking this!

4 When over half the stock has been soaked up, add half of the beer followed immediately by more stock (don't add the beer to a dry pan). Add the remainder of the beer with the last of the stock.

5 When the pearl barley or rice is cooked, stir in the Cheddar and Parmesan cheeses and remove the pan from the heat.

6 Leave the risotto to relax in the pan for a minute or two before serving with lots of black pepper.

BEER STYLE: PALE ALE

EAT IT WITH...
Try a glass of really fruity, smooth Pale Ale such as Firestone Walker Pale 31, Lagunitas DayTime, or Beavertown Neck Oil; it lifts all the fruity flavors in the cheese and loves the sweetness in the onions. The bitterness also helps cut through the richness.

SAISON-SPIKED FISH LAKSA

When you apply heat to beer the first elements you tend to lose are the volatile aromas, and then the bitterness barges in, which is often an unwelcome double-play. To bypass that, you can use beer as an additional seasoning and this Laksa, which is a curried noodle soup, adds an aromatic Saison (like Brooklyn's Sorachi Ace) as if it's a squeeze of lime at the end of cooking. By doing this you get to keep the aroma, plus some of the yeast's spicy qualities, and you still get the richness of malt and alcohol—the added bonus is that you only add a small amount of beer and can drink the rest with dinner.

SERVES 4

FOR THE SPICE PASTE

3 garlic cloves, chopped

1in (2.5cm) piece of fresh ginger, peeled and roughly chopped

4 scallions (spring onions), roughly chopped

1–2 red chili peppers, roughly chopped

2 lemon grass stalks, outer layer removed and very finely chopped

1 teaspoon ground turmeric

2 teaspoons curry powder

½ teaspoon five spice

1 tablespoon Thai fish sauce

1 teaspoon soft brown sugar

FOR THE LAKSA

Coconut or groundnut oil, for frying

1 red bell (sweet) pepper, sliced

Handful of chopped green beans or asparagus

14fl oz (400ml) can coconut milk

¾ cup (200ml) hot fish, chicken, or vegetable stock

10½oz (300g) flat rice noodles (or cooked white rice)

7oz (200g) peeled raw shrimps (prawns)

5oz (150g) cooked crabmeat (canned is fine)

4 tablespoons Saison

Juice of 1 lime

Salt

Handful of fresh cilantro (coriander), to serve

1 To make the spice paste, blitz all the ingredients in a blender until thick and smooth—this will take a few minutes.

2 To make the laksa, fry the paste in the oil over a medium heat in a large wok or frying pan for a few minutes before adding the red pepper and green beans or asparagus.

3 Pour in the coconut milk and stock, and simmer for 5 minutes.

4 Meanwhile, prepare the rice noodles according to the instructions on the packet—often this will just involve soaking in boiling water. An alternative is to cook white rice.

5 Add the shrimps (prawns) and crabmeat to the curried coconut broth and simmer for up to 5 minutes, or until the fish is cooked through. (Alternatively, you could use cooked chicken pieces or tofu.)

6 Remove from the heat, and add the beer and lime juice. Check the taste: you may want to add more fish sauce, salt, lime, beer, or chili, according to taste.

7 To serve, place the cooked noodles or rice in large bowls. Pour the curried fish broth over the top and sprinkle with the fresh cilantro (coriander).

SERVES 4

FOR THE LEFTOVER LAGER CURRY

2 white onions, roughly chopped
Butter, for frying
2 garlic cloves, finely chopped
1–2 red chili peppers, finely chopped
A thumb-sized piece of fresh ginger, peeled and finely chopped
1 teaspoon ground cumin
1 teaspoon ground coriander
1 teaspoon ground turmeric
½ teaspoon cayenne pepper
½ teaspoon fennel seeds
½ teaspoon ground cardamom (or 6 whole pods, crushed)
1 cinnamon stick
6–8 chicken thighs, skinned, boned, and cubed (or an equivalent amount of diced vegetables for a vegetarian alternative)
4 fresh plum tomatoes, chopped
2 cups (500ml) lager
4 tablespoons natural yogurt
Fresh cilantro (coriander), to garnish
Salt and black pepper

FOR THE LAGER RICE

2 cups (400g) basmati rice
1½ cups (375ml) water
½ cup (125ml) lager
1 teaspoon salt
1 teaspoon ground turmeric
4 cardamom pods

FOR THE LAGER CHAPATI

2 cups (250g) wholewheat (wholemeal) flour (or self-raising flour to turn the chapati into roti), plus extra for dusting
½ teaspoon salt
⅓ cup (100ml) lager
¼ cup (50ml) water

LEFTOVER LAGER CURRY
WITH LAGER RICE AND LAGER CHAPATI

Do you have the kind of friends who bring crap beer to your house? Or have you ever had a couple of cans of lager in the fridge that you just don't want to drink? If so, this is the most delicious way to maximize these tasteless brews and turn them into a tasty feast.

1   To make the chapati dough, combine the flour and salt in a bowl, gradually pour in the lager, and then the water. Mix together until you have a thick dough. Knead the dough for 5 minutes and then set to one side.

2   To make the curry, sweat the onion in some butter in a large saucepan for 5 minutes. Add the garlic, chili, and ginger, and stir for a couple of minutes.

3   Add all the spices and season with salt and black pepper. Allow the spices to cook into the onion mix for a few minutes, but be careful that the contents of the pan don't burn. Add the chicken thighs (or vegetables) and cook for 5–8 minutes.

4   Add the tomatoes, pour in the lager, and then simmer for 15–20 minutes.

5   Take off the heat. Remove the cinnamon stick and stir in the yogurt. Cover and leave the curry in the pan until you're ready to serve.

6   To make the rice, rinse the grains in a sieve for a few minutes and place in a saucepan. Add the remaining ingredients and bring to a boil. Once boiling, turn the heat down as low as it will go, put a lid on the pan, and cook for around 10 minutes, or until the rice has absorbed all the liquid. Stir with a fork and remove the cardamom pods (or warn people that they're there).

7   While the curry and rice are cooking, take the chapati/roti dough and knead for a further minute. Dust the work surface with some flour and cut the dough into 8 separate balls. Use a rolling pin to flatten out the balls until they are very thin.

8   Cook one of the chapatis in a dry frying pan for around 30 seconds. Flip the chapati over and cook on the other side for another 30 seconds. Repeat for all the chapatis and then place them in a low oven until needed.

EAT IT WITH...

This kind of curry is ideal with a lager, but not the one that you cooked with. Instead, go for something unfiltered or, even better, a great Dunkel, which works well to cool down the heat, loves the spices, and gives a hint of sweetness. It's especially good with the chapati. Try New Belgium 1554 or a classic Munich Dunkel like Ayinger or Paulaner.

SERVES 4-6

2 celery sticks, finely chopped

1 red onion, finely chopped

Olive oil, for frying

2 garlic cloves, finely chopped

3½oz (100g) mushrooms, diced

2 medium zucchini (courgettes), diced

2 medium carrots, peeled and diced

14oz (400g) can green lentils

14oz (400g) can chopped tomatoes

¾ cup (200ml) Bock

1 teaspoon fresh thyme leaves

Salt and black pepper

FOR THE POTATO TOPPING

2¼lb (1kg) potatoes, peeled and roughly chopped

2oz (50g) blue cheese

¼ cup (50ml) Bock

¼ cup (50ml) milk

Salt and black pepper

BOCK, BLUE CHEESE, AND VEGETABLE COTTAGE PIE

This is traditional British home cooking, the kind I grew up eating, only adapted to be vegetarian and including blue cheese and Bock, a strong and malty lager that's excellent with slow-cooked vegetables. It's a dinner that you eat with a spoon on a cold winter's night and is the equivalent of a big food hug.

1 Soften the celery and onion in some olive oil and then add the garlic. After a few minutes, stir in the mushrooms, zucchini (courgettes), and carrots.

2 Add the lentils, tomatoes, beer, and thyme, season with salt and black pepper, and simmer for 30 minutes.

3 To make the potato topping, boil the potatoes until soft (around 10 minutes) in a saucepan of salted water.

4 Drain the potatoes and place them in a dry pan. Add the blue cheese, beer, and milk, and mash together until smooth with some additional seasoning, if desired.

5 Preheat the oven to 400°F/200°C/Gas 6. Spread the vegetable mix over the bottom of a large baking dish, then spread the mashed potato over the top.

6 Cook the pie in the oven for 15–20 minutes or until golden and bubbling (you could prepare the dish the night before, keep in the refrigerator, and then heat through for 30–40 minutes, or until hot all the way through).

BEER STYLE: PORTER

EAT IT WITH...

You could drink the Bock with this, but I prefer a Porter for its drier finish and darker depth of malt. Try Deschutes Black Butte, Sam Smith Taddy Porter, or Renaissance Elemental Porter from New Zealand.

VEGETABLE CRUMBLE

Crumble is one of my favorite puddings, but this recipe turns it into a savory vegetable version, which can either work on its own or as a side dish with some roasted meat or sausages. I like to use Belgian Dubbel or a Dark Lager in this recipe, because you need something low in bitterness and with a little sweetness.

SERVES 4-6

FOR THE FILLING

Around 1½lb (700g) vegetables (I use cauliflower, parsnips, carrots, leeks, potatoes, and broccoli)

2 tablespoons butter

2 tablespoons all-purpose (plain) flour

¾ cup (200ml) hot vegetable stock

1 tablespoon Dijon mustard

¾ cup (200ml) Dubbel or Dark Lager

Sea salt and black pepper, to season

FOR THE TOPPING

4 tablespoons (50g) butter

Scant 1 cup (100g) all-purpose (plain) flour

½ cup (50g) rolled oats

Scant 1 cup (100g) grated Cheddar cheese

1 teaspoon fresh thyme leaves

Sea salt and black pepper

1 To make the filling, dice all the vegetables into ½in (1cm) cubes, then parboil in salted water for around 10 minutes (or until just soft in the center). Drain and place in a large baking dish. Preheat the oven to 375°F/190°C/Gas 5.

2 Melt the butter in a saucepan, then whisk in the flour to make a roux. Gradually add the stock followed by the mustard. Stir for 5 minutes until the sauce thickens. Remove from the heat and add the beer, mixing until combined. Pour the sauce over the vegetables in the dish.

3 To make the topping, use your fingers to rub the butter into the flour until the mixture resembles breadcrumbs.

4 Add the oats, Cheddar cheese, and thyme, and season with sea salt and black pepper. Mix together.

5 Sprinkle over the crumble topping and bake in the oven for around 30 minutes, or until golden and bubbling.

BEER STYLE:
BELGIAN DUBBEL

EAT IT WITH...

This is a good all-rounder of a dish. The butter and cheese on top, plus the bitter-sweet vegetables, are all pleasing flavors with beer. A Belgian Dubbel, such as Westmalle Dubbel, is a nice choice, with the toasty sweetness and subtle spice working really well. The savory stock base also makes this a nice match for an English-style Pale Ale—try Marston's Pedigree or Timothy Taylor's Landlord.

CHAPTER 4

ULTIMATE MEALS

BEER CHEESE SAUCE

Spread this on the burger too, taking inspiration from the Rarebit Burger on page 105.

BEER BRIOCHE BUNS

These hold the whole thing together with their soft sweetness—check out the recipe on page 114.

BEER KETCHUP

Add this to the underside of the bun—just follow the recipe for Weizen Ketchup on page 34. You can also add some Beer Mustard if you wish (see page 118).

EXTRAS

Not enough for you? Then add some Snakebite Pickles (see page 36), some DIPA Mayo (see page 60), some Smoked Beer Pulled Pork (see page 90), and serve with Beer-baked Fries (see page 34).

THE ULTIMATE BEER BURGER

What is the ultimate beer-infused burger? In how many ways is it possible to get beer inside your burger experience? The answer is lots. This burger is served inside beer brioche buns. It includes beer ketchup, beer cheese sauce, beer onions, and beer-cured bacon. The only thing not using any beer is the actual meat itself—you can add beer to the meat patty, of course, but, when you've got great beef, then all you really need is salt and pepper. This is the ultimate beer burger.

BEER ONIONS

1 red onion
1 tablespoon butter
1 teaspoon brown sugar
2 tablespoons Dark Beer (Dunkel Lager, Porter, Stout, or Dubbel are best)
Salt and black pepper

Peel the onion, cut in half, then cut the halves into thin semicircles. Put the butter in a pan over a low heat, add the onions and sugar, season with salt and black pepper, and cook slowly until the onions are caramelized and soft. Add the beer in the last few minutes and cook until everything reduces to a thick, soft, sweet pile of onions.

BEER-CARAMELIZED BACON

2 bacon rashers
1 tablespoon sugar
1 tablespoon Porter

Place the bacon on a baking tray. Cover with the sugar and beer. Bake in the oven on a high heat for 10 minutes, or until dark and caramelized.

EAT IT WITH...

I always think IPA is the best with a burger. The hops are great with the fruitiness in the condiments, while the bitterness can rip right through the richness of the meat and cheese. Bear Republic's Racer 5 has long been a favorite of mine. Moor Beer Co. Hoppiness is brilliant, as is Birra del Borgo's ReAle Extra or Tuatara APA from New Zealand.

THE ULTIMATE BEER CHEESE SAUCE

4 tablespoons (50g) butter

3 tablespoons all-purpose (plain) flour

1 teaspoon English mustard powder (or the actual mustard)

1²⁄₃ cup (400ml) whole milk

1¼ cup (150g) grated cheese (a mix of Cheddar cheese, Parmesan cheese, and Gouda is excellent)

A few splashes of Worcestershire sauce (optional)

1 tablespoon natural yogurt (optional)

²⁄₃ cup (150ml) beer

Salt and white and/or black pepper

This is the only beer cheese sauce you'll ever need. The beauty of a sauce such as this is its versatility, especially if you adjust the amounts of liquid you add to make it thicker or thinner. I've made it with a variety of different beers: Pale Ales can work well–just watch out for too much bitterness; nice malty Märzen lagers are good; Stout and Porter are nice, where you'll want low roast and bitterness. My preference is for Belgian beer, with Blondes, Ambers, or Dubbels all being excellent choices. The base recipe here is designed for mac 'n' cheese. The varients on page 105 use the same process, just different quantities for the ingredients.

1 Melt the butter in a large saucepan over a medium heat, add the flour and mustard powder, and whisk for a few minutes to create a thick roux.

2 Gradually add the milk, stirring constantly, until the sauce thickens and continue stirring until it's smooth.

3 Turn down the heat as low as it will go and add the remainder of the ingredients (reserving some of the grated cheese), saving the beer until last. (If you're adding yogurt, you'll find that it gives the sauce a refreshing lift.) Check the seasoning and adjust according to taste.

BEER STYLE: IPA

EAT IT WITH...

This is one of those recipes that rocks with many different beers, from Best Bitter through Pale Ales, and up to strong, dark Belgian Dubbels. I really like an IPA with a classic mac 'n' cheese, whereas a cauliflower cheese wants less bitterness, so a Dubbel is better.

FOR BEER MAC 'N' CHEESE AND BEER CAULIFLOWER CHEESE

Cook the macaroni (or other pasta) according to the packet instructions, but drain a minute or two early. Parboil your cauliflower (you can add some broccoli florets as well, if you wish). It's important to drain the macaroni or cauliflower/broccoli thoroughly to remove all of the water.

Place the macaroni or cauliflower (and broccoli if using) in a large baking dish, and cover with the beer cheese sauce. Combine ¾ cup (50g) of fresh breadcrumbs with some grated cheese, such as Cheddar cheese, Parmesan cheese, Gruyère, or Gouda–a handful of cheese per person is a simple rule–and sprinkle over the sauce.

I like to add a sprinkle of cayenne pepper too, but you can add many other ingredients to this, including cooked smoked bacon and leeks, as well as jalapeño chili peppers. Also try putting some crumbled blue or smoked cheese in the mix for extra oomph.

CROQUE MONSIEUR

This is the best toasted sandwich in the world and makes a perfect lunch or snack with a couple of beers. You need two slices of thick bread, some butter and Dijon mustard, thick slices of ham, plus your beer cheese sauce. The recipe for the sauce follows the same method as for The Ultimate Beer Cheese Sauce, but makes a thicker sauce. Two tips: use Dijon instead of English mustard and skip the Worcestershire sauce.

Start by toasting one side of each slice of bread. Butter the untoasted sides. Place one slice toasted side down, spread with some mustard, add a thick layer of ham, and then spread with cheese sauce. Place under the broiler (grill) for a minute or two until the topping bubbles. Remove from the broiler. Then place the other slice of bread on top (toasted side facing up) and cover with more cheese sauce. Broil (grill) again until the sauce bubbles and turns thick. Add a fried egg to make it a Croque Madame.

SERVES 2

2 tablespoons (25g) butter

1 tablespoon plain flour

1 teaspoon English mustard powder (or the actual mustard)

⅔ cup (150ml) whole milk

1 cup (100g) grated cheese (make sure you include some Cheddar cheese)

A few splashes of Worcestershire sauce

5 tablespoons beer

Salt and white and/or black pepper

BEER STYLE:
BIÈRE DE GARDE

EAT IT WITH...
I like something golden, strong, and Belgian or French with this. A classic Bière de Garde like La Gavroche is excellent for its sweetness and dry finish, or have a modern Tripel from Brasserie de la Senne, whose Jambe-de-Bois is a hoppy little Belgian beauty.

WELSH RAREBIT

The best cheese on toast ever. For the beer cheese sauce, follow the ingredient quantities given for Croque Monsieur, but use a British Ale or Porter for the beer and add a few extra splashes of Worcestershire sauce. Toast a thick slice of bread on one side. Flip it over, layer on the beer cheese sauce, and toast again until the topping bubbles and browns.

FOR RAREBIT BURGER
Drawing on the same idea as a Welsh Rarebit, make a beer cheese sauce using a Pale Ale or Brown Ale and add some fresh chili peppers or even some cooked bacon at the end, if you wish. Layer the beer cheese sauce onto a burger and broil (grill) just before serving.

BEER STYLE:
ENGLISH ALE

EAT THESE WITH...
Have a classic English Ale, something bitter and malty like Fuller's London Pride or Timothy Taylor's Landlord. A good glass of Mild also works well as the chocolatey dark malt is excellent with the rich cheese.

THE ULTIMATE BEER PIZZA

If a baking recipe calls for a liquid, then you can add beer. In a pizza dough the addition of a malty, slightly sweet lager gives a great caramelized depth. Top that with a simple beer tomato sauce and then load on your beer-infused toppings, which includes a beer pesto–I don't think you can beat basil and Parmesan cheese on a pizza, so this just adapts that idea. And always, always put lots of fresh mozzarella on top.

MAKES 6-8 PIZZAS

FOR THE BEER TOMATO SAUCE

2 x 14oz (400g) cans good-quality tomatoes
2 garlic cloves, finely chopped
1 teaspoon each salt, sugar, and black pepper
4 tablespoons Dark Lager
1 tablespoon olive oil
Small bunch of freshly torn basil leaves

FOR THE BEER PIZZA

1¼ cups (300ml) lukewarm water
1 tablespoon superfine (caster) sugar
2 x ¼oz (7g) sachets fast-action dried yeast
4 tablespoons olive oil
1 bottle of Dark Lager, at room temperature
2¼lb (1kg) Tipo "00" flour or strong white bread flour, plus extra for dusting
1 teaspoon sea salt
Selection of pizza toppings (including plenty of mozzarella)
Black pepper

TO MAKE THE TOMATO SAUCE

1 Simmer all the ingredients in a saucepan until the sauce reduces and thickens.

TO MAKE THE PIZZA

1 Combine the water, sugar, yeast, and olive oil in a jug, stirring everything together to activate the yeast. Leave for a few minutes and then add the beer (it's a good idea to pour this into a glass in advance to let it go flat).

2 Sift the flour and salt onto a clean work surface and make a large well in the middle.

3 Gradually pour the yeast-beer mix into the well, using a fork to bring the mixture together until you can hold it in your hands. Knead the dough for a few minutes, place in a large, flour-dusted bowl, then put plastic wrap (clingfilm) over the bowl and leave in a warm place for around an hour.

4 Dust a clean work surface with flour. Place the dough on the surface and punch it around a bit, knocking out the air and folding and kneading it for a few minutes. You can use the dough immediately or cover with plastic wrap (clingfilm) and keep in the refrigerator.

5 When you're ready to bake the pizza, divide the dough into 6-8 balls and roll out flat. Place a thin layer of tomato sauce on top of each pizza and then add the remainder of your toppings, including the Beer Pesto, and plenty of freshly torn mozzarella and black pepper.

6 To bake, turn the oven to the highest setting (around 480°F/250°C/Gas 8, unless you've got a badass oven) and place a tray in the oven to preheat. (Ideally, use a pizza stone or a specific pizza tray.) Bake the pizza in the oven for 8-10 minutes or until golden and crisp.

BEER PESTO

Add a large handful of freshly torn basil leaves and ½ cup (50g) grated Parmesan cheese to a mixing bowl. Pour in 2 tablespoons beer (Dark Lager or Saison is good) and 2 tablespoons extra virgin olive oil, followed by 1 peeled garlic clove. Put the ingredients in a blender and blitz until thick and smooth.

BEER STYLE:
PILSNER

EAT IT WITH...

It's pizza, which I think we can agree goes with almost every beer. Keep it a little bit authentic, though, by choosing Italy's first beer style: the Italian Pilsner. The main qualities of this beer are that it's clean, dry, bitter, and aromatic from being dry-hopped—and those hops love garlic and basil. Try Birrificio Italiano's Tipopils, Firestone Walker's Pivo Pils, or Fourpure's Dry Hopped Pils.

THE ULTIMATE BEER QUESADILLA

Whether drinking, drunk, or hungover, quesadillas are a brilliant beer food. By layering tortillas, meat, salsa, guacamole, and lots of cheese, and then baking it all, you get a kind of Mexican pizza sandwich. A dark Mexican lager such as Negra Modelo works in all these recipes.

CHEESE

The cheese is obviously the important bit (it's the quesa part)—you can add a thick Beer Cheese Sauce (see page 104) using lots of Cheddar cheese, Monterey Jack, and some queso, or just simply cover everything in grated cheese.

The recipes given here will make three to four quesadillas and it's simply a matter of stacking the ingredients on a baking tray—so a tortilla first, then the brined beef, lager salsa, guacamole, cheese, and finally another cooked tortilla—before baking at 400°F/200°C/Gas 6 for 10 minutes.

BEER-BRINED BEEF

Use 1 flank steak per person. Follow the brine instructions for Beer Hot Wings on page 40, using a Dark Lager or Porter, and add a teaspoon of ground cumin. Leave for 8–24 hours. To cook, slice the steak into thin strips then fry in olive oil for 5–10 minutes.

GUACAMOLE

In a large bowl, smash together a ripe avocado, the juice of ½ lime, ½ finely diced white onion, ½ green chili, 1 teaspoon of salt, and 2 tablespoons of beer. Mix until thick and smooth.

BEER TORTILLAS

Tortillas (and tacos) are so easy—and cheap—to make. Just take 2 heaping cups (250g) of masa harina flour, a bottle of beer, and some salt, mix them together, and let rest for 15 minutes. Roll out the tortillas until they are thin (or place in a taco press), then griddle in a dry pan for 30 seconds on each side.

TOMATO LAGER SALSA

Take 7oz (200g) of fresh cherry tomatoes, ½ red onion, and a green chili pepper (or two if you like it hot) and cut them up as finely as you can (especially the onion and chili). Combine everything in a bowl with a teaspoon each of sugar, salt, and black pepper, and then 2 tablespoons of beer. You could also roast your ingredients for 20 minutes on a medium heat before blitzing.

EAT IT WITH...

A Dark Lager or subtle Dark Ale are great choices, as they can work with all the different flavors and textures and not let anything overpower—nor will the beer overpower anything. New Belgium 1554 or Budvar Dark are both good, or something like Aussie White Rabbit Dark Ale, which has a nice dried fruitiness.

CHAPTER 5

BAKING

CLASSIC BEER BREAD

My suspicion is that beer bread came about centuries ago when baking and brewing were both routine household tasks and the yeast from the brewing pot was simply scooped off the top and added to the flour to create bread dough—that seems a logical assumption to me and would make it one of the oldest forms of cooking with beer. The benefit of baking with beer is that you get some additional yeast, plus extra sugar, both good things in a dough. I prefer to bake things such as pretzels and fast doughs (like flatbreads), but this makes a decent loaf, where the best advice is just to avoid hop bitterness because no one wants to eat bitter bread—Wheat Beer, Helles, Dunkel, and sweet Stouts are best.

MAKES 1 LOAF

⅔ cup (150ml) whole milk

1 tablespoon (15g) butter, plus extra for greasing

1 tablespoon malt extract (or white sugar)

¼oz (7g) sachet dried fast-action yeast

¾ cup (200ml) beer, at room temperature

5 cups (500g) strong bread flour (white or wholewheat/wholemeal— I prefer the latter), plus extra for dusting

1 teaspoon sea salt

1 Gently warm the milk, butter, and malt extract or sugar in a saucepan until the butter melts—don't allow the liquid to boil. Allow to cool until lukewarm. Pour into a mixing bowl and stir in the yeast. Leave for 5 minutes, then add most of the beer (reserving some). Leave for another 5 minutes.

2 Add the flour and salt to the bowl and combine the wet and dry ingredients to form a smooth dough (adding more beer if the dough is too dry). Lightly flour the work surface and turn out the dough. Knead for 5–10 minutes. Return the dough to the bowl, cover with plastic wrap (clingfilm), and place in a warm place for 1 hour (or until the dough has roughly doubled in size).

3 Grease a medium-sized bread tin with butter. Place the dough on a floured work surface and knock it about a few times. Place the dough in the prepared tin, cover with a damp dishtowel (tea towel), and allow to rise for about 30 minutes.

4 Preheat the oven to 425°F/220°C/Gas 7. Bake the bread in the oven, reducing the heat to 350°F/180°C/Gas 4 after 10 minutes, before baking for a further 25–30 minutes or until the bread is golden brown (and sounds hollow when you tap the base of the loaf). Leave to cool on a wire rack.

BEER BRIOCHE BUNS

MAKES 10-12

3 tablespoons lukewarm milk

½oz (10g) fast-action dried yeast

⅓ cup (100ml) Hefeweizen (at room temperature)

3 tablespoons superfine (caster) sugar

5 cups (500g) strong white bread flour, plus extra for dusting

7 tablespoons (100g) butter

1 teaspoon sea salt

3 eggs, beaten, plus 1 extra beaten egg to glaze

Sweet and light, yet a little chewy, brioche is my favorite bun for a burger, where it somehow has the ability to melt into the meat. As with all dough, this calls for liquid and adding beer works well. I use Hefeweizen (it's a favorite style of mine for baking), but you could use Oatmeal Stout or something similarly low in bitterness. And these buns work with whatever you want to put in them, with burgers, Beer Fish Fingers (see page 54), and Smoked Beer Pulled Pork (see page 90) all being good options.

1 Mix the milk with the yeast in a jug, then add the beer and sugar. Stir gently and leave for 10 minutes.

2 Place the flour and salt in a bowl, then use your fingers to rub in the butter until the mixture resembles breadcrumbs. Add 3 of the beaten eggs and the beer-yeast mix, combine into a dough, and knead for 10 minutes on a floured work surface. Put the dough in a large, flour-dusted bowl, cover with plastic wrap (clingfilm), and leave in a warm place for 1–3 hours (the dough should roughly double in size).

3 Line a baking tray with baking paper. Take the dough and knead for 2 minutes, then divide into 10–12 pieces. Roll each piece individually into a neat ball and place on the tray. Cover and leave for 1 hour—the dough balls will rise again.

4 Preheat the oven to 400°F/200°C/Gas 6 and place a tray on the bottom shelf. Glaze each bun with the final beaten egg. Take a glass of water and pour this into the tray at the bottom of the oven when you bake the buns to create some steam. Bake for 15–20 minutes until lightly golden—the buns are ready when the base makes a hollow sound when tapped. Leave to cool on a wire rack, then put a massive burger inside each one.

IPA AND HONEY CORNBREAD

MAKES 1 LOAF

7 tablespoons (100g) butter
Scant 1 cup (150g) coarse cornmeal
¾ cup (100g) all-purpose (plain) flour
2 tablespoons soft light brown sugar
1 teaspoon baking powder
Pinch of baking soda (bicarbonate of soda)
1 teaspoon sea salt
2 large eggs, beaten
⅔ cup (160ml) whole milk
5 tablespoons (75ml) IPA or Double IPA
2 tablespoons honey

1 Preheat the oven to 425°F/220°C/Gas7. In a pan, melt 4 tablespoons (50g) of the butter and set to one side to cool.

2 Combine all the dry ingredients in a bowl and mix the wet ingredients in a jug, reserving the unmelted butter. Pour the liquid into the dry ingredients, and stir.

3 Melt the remaining butter in a heavy skillet pan. Ensure the butter is hot (you could also use pig fat instead), then pour the batter on top of the butter. (If you don't have a skillet, then use a 9in/23cm cake tin or baking dish: simply heat the butter in a pan, pour it into the batter, then put everything in the tin or dish.)

4 Bake the cornbread in the oven for 25–35 minutes, or until golden brown.

BEER CRACKERS

Why buy crackers when you can cook them yourself and add a favorite beer into the mix? Go with a beer that's got plenty of malt depth and low bitterness—Oatmeal Stout is ideal, or try a sweet Barley Wine or Quadrupel. You can also add a handful of grated cheese to the crackers or mix in some seeds.

MAKES 10-12

2 cups (250g) wholewheat (wholemeal) flour, plus extra for dusting
2 tablespoons (25g) dark brown sugar
½ teaspoon baking soda (bicarbonate of soda)
½ teaspoon salt
1 stick (125g) butter (at room temperature), plus extra for greasing
2 tablespoons Stout
Milk, for glazing

1 Preheat the oven to 325°F/170°C/Gas 3.

2 Combine all the dry ingredients in a large bowl and then use your fingers to rub in the butter until the mixture resembles breadcrumbs. Add the beer and combine until you have a dough.

3 Dust the work surface with flour and then roll out the dough until it's about ¼in (5mm) thick.

4 Cut the dough into squares or rectangles, and place on a greased baking tray. Prick the surface of the crackers with a fork and glaze with milk. Bake in the oven for 25–30 minutes.

2 cups (250g) wholewheat (wholemeal) flour, plus extra for dusting

1 teaspoon salt

1 teaspoon baking soda (bicarbonate of soda)

1 tablespoon honey

⅔ cup (150ml) beer

⅓ cup (100ml) buttermilk or natural yogurt

Plus your selection of additional ingredients (see below)

BEER SODA BREAD

Soda bread is the quickest and easiest loaf to put together if you want some bread to go with dinner or, even better, to go with cheese and meats. The basic recipe is also ideal for experimenting with different beers and other ingredients, especially as it's a forgiving loaf that doesn't need the same kind of care as a yeast-risen bread. I have two favorite versions: one savory (Cheese, Onion, and Porter) and the other sweet (Dried Fruit and Dubbel).

1   Preheat the oven to 400°F/200°C/Gas 6.

2   Mix all the dry ingredients in one bowl and all the wet ingredients in another. Then pour the wet ingredients into the dry ones, and mix together well, eventually using your hands to form the mixture into a bread dough.

3   Knead the dough for a few minutes on a floured work surface, shape into a round loaf, and place on a baking tray. Score a large cross in the top of the loaf. Bake in the oven for around 45 minutes. To check if the bread is ready, turn the loaf over and tap the base—if it's done, it'll sound hollow.

RECIPE VARIATIONS:

CHEESE, ONION, AND PORTER

Add ¾ cup (75g) grated Cheddar cheese to the bread dough (reserving some to sprinkle on top of the loaf). Use some Porter for the beer element. Finely chop some rings of red onion and arrange them on top of the loaf before baking. Finally, sprinkle with a few sprigs of rosemary to serve.

DRIED FRUIT AND DUBBEL

Into the dough, add ½ cup (75g) of mixed dried fruit and a teaspoon each of ground cinnamon and ground nutmeg. Use a Belgian Dubbel as the beer. Sprinkle some brown sugar over the top of the loaf before baking.

SOFT BEER PRETZEL BITES
WITH BEER MUSTARD

We all love pretzels, right? They have the ideal composition for a beer snack: they're dough-based, able to absorb some alcohol, and have a saltiness that makes you thirstier. I use Hefeweizen in this recipe, as it gives a little hint of sweetness that works very well. They are best eaten on the day they're made and topping them with cheese is a great addition. The beer mustard is super-easy and best made in advance, since it mellows over time. These are bites because rolling pretzels is surprisingly complicated. Feel free to roll them properly if you want to be more authentic–the process is exactly the same; you might just need to add 5 minutes to the cooking time.

MAKES 25-30

FOR THE PRETZEL BITES

1 tablespoon malt extract (or soft brown sugar)

7 cups (1.6 liters) water, plus ⅓ cup (100ml) extra

2 x ¼oz (7g) sachets fast-action dried yeast

⅔ cup (160ml) Hefeweizen (at room temperature)

4 cups (500g) all-purpose (plain) flour, plus extra for dusting

2 teaspoons sea salt, plus extra for sprinkling on top

6 tablespoons (80g) butter

3 tablespoons baking soda (bicarbonate of soda)

FOR THE BEER MUSTARD

Heaping ½ cup (100g) mustard seeds (a mix of yellow and black is good)

⅓ cup (100ml) beer (I like Pilsner or Wheat Beer)

¼ cup (50ml) cider vinegar

1 teaspoon white sugar (or malt extract or honey)

Sea salt and black pepper

1. To make the pretzels, mix the malt extract, ⅓ cup (100ml) of warm water, and the yeast in a jug. Leave for 5 minutes, then add the beer and leave for a further 5 minutes–this is to activate the yeast.

2. Mix the flour and salt in a bowl, then use your fingers to rub the butter into the flour until the mixture resembles breadcrumbs.

3. Gradually add the liquid from the jug and combine into a dough. Knead the dough on a floured work surface for around 10 minutes, then roll into a ball, place in a large, flour-dusted bowl, cover with plastic wrap (clingfilm), and leave to rest for 1–2 hours.

4. Knead for a further minute and then cut the dough into 6 equal pieces. Roll the pieces into long, fat sausages (about 1in/2.5cm in diameter), then divide into roughly golf-ball-sized bites. Place the bites on a tray and leave to rest for 30 minutes in a warm place, then for 30 minutes somewhere cold–the refrigerator is fine.

5. Preheat the oven to 400°F/200°C/Gas 6). Take a large baking tray (or two) and line with baking paper.

6. Boil 7 cups (1.6 liters) of water in a large pan and add the baking soda (bicarbonate of soda), but be careful as it'll erupt and bubble violently for a brief time–so only add a spoon at a time. Dip the dough bites, a few at a time, in the boiling water for 20 seconds, stirring them once, then place on the lined baking tray. Sprinkle the bites with salt (and some cheese, if you like) and bake for around 15 minutes or until deep golden. Leave to cool on a wire rack.

7. To make the mustard, place the mustard seeds in a bowl and pour over the beer and vinegar. Cover and place in the refrigerator for 24–48 hours. Place in a hand-blender, along with the sugar, sea salt, and black pepper (to taste), and blitz into a smooth texture. Pimp this however you wish–adding herbs, spices, and different beers can change the mustard.

EAT IT WITH...

A pretzel in one hand and a big glass of Helles in the other. That's all you need. And, of course, this works with any beer, but there's something perfect about having it with German lager. Take your pick, but my top choices are Augustiner Edelstoff and Tegernseer Spezial or, if you can't get German, then Jack's Abby Jabby Brau or Lovedale Lager.

CHAPTER 6

SWEET THINGS

DOUBLE IPA CARROT CAKE

This is the best cake I've ever made. Double IPA is an amazing match for carrot cake, so I thought I'd use it in this recipe, where it gives a kick of citrus that is especially noticeable and nice in the frosting. Use the fruitiest and most aromatic beer you can find.

SERVES 8–10

½ cup (75g) raisins or sultanas

3oz (75g) sliced pineapple (fresh or canned)

¼ cup (50ml) Double IPA

1¾ sticks (200g) butter (at room temperature), plus extra for greasing

1 cup (200g) light brown sugar

4 egg yolks

Pinch of salt

Zest of 1 orange

Scant 2 cups (225g) self-raising flour (white or wholewheat/wholemeal)

1 teaspoon baking powder

½ teaspoon each ground cinnamon and ground ginger

9oz (250g) carrots, grated and squeezed of juice

FOR THE CAKE FROSTING

10½oz (300g) full fat cream cheese

7oz (200g) mascarpone cheese

¼ cup (50ml) Double IPA

Zest of 1 orange

Confectioners' (icing) sugar, to taste

1 Preheat the oven to 350°F/180°C/Gas 4. In a bowl, soak the raisins and pineapple in the Double IPA.

2 In a large bowl, cream together the butter and sugar. Mix in the egg yolks, salt, and orange zest.

3 Fold in the flour, baking powder, cinnamon, and ginger.

4 Mix in the carrots, followed by the raisin, pineapple, and beer mixture, and combine well.

5 Pour the cake mixture into two 10in (25cm) greased and lined cake tins. Bake in the oven for about 30–35 minutes. Check if the cakes are ready by pushing a skewer into the middle and seeing if it comes out clean–the cakes may need an extra 5–10 minutes. Remove the cakes from the oven and allow to cool before turning out onto a wire cooling rack.

6 To make the frosting, mix together the cheeses, beer, and orange zest. Stir in the sugar a little at a time (starting with 1 tablespoon) until it has the sweetness you want.

7 Sandwich the two cakes together with frosting and spread more frosting on top.

8 Cut yourself an enormous slice of cake, pour a beer, and enjoy.

EAT IT WITH...

An IPA or Double IPA, of course. Try Firestone Walker Double Jack, Thornbridge Halcyon, or Epic Brewing's Hop Zombie. These are perfect with this cake.

EAT IT WITH...

Ideally you want an Imperial Stout that's been aged in Bourbon barrels—you need a powerful beer to handle the chocolate and banana. Opt for New Holland's Dragon's Milk or BrewDog Paradox, or look for Siren's regular barrel-aged brews.

STOUT CHOCOLATE BANANA PUDDING

Butter, for greasing
4 bananas, cut into rings
6 tablespoons maple syrup
Scant 1 cup (100g) self-raising flour
½ cup (60g) cocoa powder
3oz (75g) suet (regular or vegetable)
½ cup (100g) superfine (caster) sugar
½ teaspoon salt
⅔ cup (150ml) Imperial Stout
¼ cup (50ml) milk
Cream, to serve

When my sister and I were growing up, we were always allowed to choose what we had for dinner on our birthdays. It could be anything we wanted and my mum would make it. I always chose the same dessert–Chocolate and Banana Pudding. It was soft and gooey with banana on the bottom, then chewy, crisp, and chocolatey on top. I hadn't had it for years until I started working on these recipes, so I decided to try it with a Barrel-aged Imperial Stout and it turned into a brilliant dessert.

1 Preheat the oven to 350°F/180°C/Gas 4.

2 Grease a medium-sized baking dish with butter, arrange the banana rings over the bottom, and cover them with the maple syrup.

3 Combine all of the dry ingredients in a bowl and then mix in the beer and milk. Stir together to form a thick batter.

4 Pour the pudding mixture over the banana and bake in the oven for 30–40 minutes until a skewer comes out clean from the middle.

5 Serve the pudding hot with some cold cream. And, if you have any leftovers, then place them in the refrigerator as they will turn into a great brownie-like treat the next day.

ABBOT'S APPLE PIE

This pie was inspired by a Belgian road trip on which I visited all the Trappist breweries. At Achel they have a large cooler of cakes and pies that we ate with their Dubbel, while at Orval I ate an apple baked in spices and dried fruit. Pulling those influences together, I put them in a pie, where I use a Belgian Quadrupel (sometimes called Abt and named after the monastery's Abbot). The beer's richness of dried fruit and spice works perfectly in this triple-hit of beer cooking (filling, crust, and custard), all possible using just one bottle of Quad.

SERVES 6-8

FOR THE QUADRUPEL APPLE PIE FILLING

2 tablespoons (25g) butter

4 large cooking apples, peeled, cored, and cut into large cubes

½ cup (100g) soft brown sugar

Pinch each of ground cinnamon and ground nutmeg

4 tablespoons Quadrupel

FOR THE QUADRUPEL PIE (SHORTCRUST) PASTRY

Follow the pie (shortcrust) pastry recipe for the Mini Beef and Beer Pies (see page 52), but use Quadrupel for the beer and add a teaspoon of sugar and a pinch of ground cinnamon to the dough. You will also need a beaten egg to glaze and some Demerara sugar for sprinkling over the finished pie.

FOR THE QUADRUPEL CUSTARD

4 tablespoons Quadrupel

1⅔ cup (400ml) whole milk

⅓ cup (100ml) single cream

1 vanilla bean (pod), split in half and seeds scraped out

6 egg yolks

2 tablespoons superfine (caster) sugar

1 To make the pie filling, melt the butter in a large pan and add the apples, sugar, spices, and beer. Stir well, put the lid on the pan, and cook for 15 minutes. Remove from the heat and allow to cool. (If you wish, you can make the pie filling and pastry a day in advance).

2 When you're ready to bake the pie, preheat the oven to 350°F/180°C/Gas 4 and grease a 8in (20cm) pie dish with some butter.

3 Make the pastry (see page 52). Roll out the pastry until it is about ¼in (5mm) thick and cut in half. Line the pie dish with one half of the pastry. Pour in the pie filling and then gently lay the other half of pastry on top. Trim and then fork or crimp the edges of the pie. Cut a small cross in the top of the pie, glaze with the beaten egg, and sprinkle with Demerara sugar. Bake in the oven for 40–45 minutes or until golden.

4 To make the custard, pour the beer into a mug and allow it to go flat (swirling the mug around will help with this).

5 Heat the milk and cream in a saucepan over a low heat. Add the vanilla bean (pod) and bring to a gentle simmer.

6 Beat the egg yolks and sugar in a large heatproof bowl.

7 Remove the vanilla bean (pod) from the pan and then gradually pour the milk and cream into the egg and sugar mix, stirring constantly with a large whisk.

8 Place a clean saucepan on the stovetop over a very low heat and then pour in the custard, stirring continuously with a wooden spoon. Once the custard has thickened, add the beer and stir to combine. Serve the pie with the custard.

EAT IT WITH...

Make sure you have an extra bottle of the beer that you used to go with this one, as that's obviously the best match. The best version I've had is made with Rochefort 10, which is like cocoa, raisins, and toasted nuts.

GRAPEFRUIT IPA PUDDING
WITH ORANGE CREAM

This is a beer-adapted version of one of my favorite desserts, which separates as it cooks to leave a super-light sponge above a layer of its own custard. It's usually made with lemons, but I use grapefruit and IPA to give a mature, sharp, and bitter pudding that is sweetened by a thick orange cream.

SERVES 6–8

FOR THE GRAPEFUIT IPA PUDDING

4 tablespoons (50g) butter, at room temperature
¾ cup (150g) superfine (caster) sugar
Pinch of salt
Zest of ½ grapefruit
Zest of ½ orange
3 eggs, separated
⅓ cup (40g) all-purpose (plain) flour
5 tablespoons grapefruit juice
5 tablespoons IPA
Scant ¾ cup (175ml) whole milk

FOR THE ORANGE CREAM

1⅔ cup (400ml) heavy (double) cream
Zest of ½ orange
2–4 tablespoons confectioners' (icing) sugar

1 Preheat the oven to 350°F/180°C/Gas 4. Butter a 2-quart (2-liter) baking dish.

2 Cream together the butter, sugar, salt, and citrus zests.

3 Mix in the egg yolks, one at a time, and then add the flour, grapefruit juice, beer, and milk a little at a time until you have a thick mixture.

4 In a separate bowl, whisk the egg whites until they form thick peaks and then fold them into the cake mixture.

5 Pour the mixture into the baking dish and stand this in a deep roasting tray. Pour boiling water into the tray until the water reaches half way up the dish. Bake in the oven for 40–45 minutes—the pudding should be sponge on top and custard-like beneath.

6 To make the orange cream, whip the heavy (double) cream with the orange zest until it is thick. Add the confectioners' (icing) sugar—2 tablespoons should be sufficient, but you may like to add more or less, according to taste.

BEER STYLE:
DOUBLE IPA

EAT IT WITH...
A Double IPA is the obvious choice, although it can be a little too much grapefruit-on-grapefruit if you don't nail it (and it can be tough to pair well with a beer). A strong Farmhouse Ale or Saison would be a good alternative here.

FOR THE PBJ CAKE

7 tablespoons (100g) butter

6oz (165g) peanut butter

1½ cups (200g) all-purpose (plain) flour

1 teaspoon baking powder

Pinch of salt

Pinch of cinnamon

1 egg

½ cup (100g) brown sugar

½ cup (120ml) beer (sweet fruit beer or Imperial Stout)

4 tablespoons (60ml) whole milk

12 teaspoons strawberry or grape jelly (jam) (or whichever flavor you prefer)

FOR THE CRUMBLE TOPPING

4 tablespoons (50g) brown sugar

4 tablespoons (50g) butter

¾ cup (100g) all-purpose (plain) flour

Pinch of salt

BEER STYLE:
IMPERIAL STOUT

EAT IT WITH...

I made the first batch of these with Fruli, the sickly sweet strawberry beer, and that was an excellent and fun match, though I do prefer the intensity of an Imperial Stout with these cakes, where a barrel-aged is even better. Choose your favorite.

PBJ CRUMBLE CAKES

My mission when writing this book was to create a recipe based on PBJ sandwiches. These cakes are salty and sweet, they contain cinnamon—which in my mind always gives them an American accent—plus I added a simple crumble topping because I wanted extra texture (and crumble toppings are awesome). There are two beer options: one is to go for a sweet fruit beer (such as Fruli, Sam Smith's version, or a sweetened Kriek), the other is to go for an Imperial Stout. Both work well.

1 Preheat the oven to 350°F/180°C/Gas 4 and line a muffin tray with muffin cases.

2 First make the crumble topping by placing all the ingredients in a bowl and using your fingers to combine them until you have a mixture resembling breadcrumbs. Set to one side.

3 To make the PBJ cake, melt together the butter and peanut butter, either in a bowl in the microwave (for just a few seconds) or on the stovetop in a saucepan over a gentle heat.

4 Combine the flour, baking powder, salt, and cinnamon in a large bowl.

5 Stir the egg, sugar, beer, and milk together in another bowl or jug until combined.

6 Mix the melted butters into the flour, then gradually add the liquid in the jug, blending everything into a thick batter.

7 Pour the batter into the muffin cases (filling each about three-quarters full), then put a teaspoon of jelly (jam) into each one.

8 Sprinkle the cakes with the crumble topping and place in the oven for around 30 minutes or until golden and cooked through.

THE BEST BEER ICE CREAMS

To make a really good beer ice cream you need to use an intensely flavored beer. To increase the flavor you can put the beer in a pan with a tablespoon of sugar and reduce it over a high heat for a few minutes to make a syrup, but only do this with beers that are very low in bitterness (or, in the case of Imperial Stout, add some additional sugar). You can use any beer, but I suggest an Imperial Stout or strong, dark Belgian beers. IPAs don't tend to work very well.

MAKES 10-12

HERE IS THE BASIC ICE CREAM RECIPE INTO WHICH YOU CAN ADD OTHER INGREDIENTS:

⅓ cup (100ml) beer
1 cup (250ml) heavy (double) cream
1 cup (250ml) whole milk
1 vanilla bean (pod), split in half and
  seeds scraped out (optional)
½ cup (100g) golden superfine
  (caster) sugar
4 egg yolks

1 Open the beer and whisk in a cup to flatten the carbonation. (To make a syrup, boil hard ⅔ cup (150ml) beer with 1 tablespoon sugar until reduced to a thick sauce.)

2 Heat the cream and milk (and optional vanilla) in a saucepan. Warm to a simmer.

3 Whisk the sugar and egg yolks together in a bowl. Remove the vanilla bean (pod) from the warm cream and very gradually pour the cream into the egg and sugar mixture, whisking constantly.

4 Pour the mixture into a clean saucepan and heat through, stirring constantly with a wooden spoon until it thickens— this takes a few minutes (if you start to get scrambled eggs, then remove from the heat and whisk like crazy).

5 When the mixture is thick, add the beer and stir through. Remove from the heat and chill before churning in an ice-cream maker.

IMPERIAL STOUT AND HOT CHOCOLATE STOUT SAUCE

Follow the recipe for basic ice cream, but use a rich, sweet Imperial Stout for the beer. Make the chocolate sauce a few minutes before you want to serve by placing 7oz (200g) of good-quality semi-sweet (dark) chocolate in a bowl over a saucepan of boiling water. Add 1 tablespoon of superfine (caster) sugar, ½ teaspoon of salt, ⅓ cup (100ml) heavy (double) cream, and, once the chocolate has melted, 4 tablespoons of Imperial Stout. Pour over the ice cream.

DUBBEL ICE CREAM

Follow the basic ice cream recipe above, adding 1 cinnamon stick to the cream, then at the end add the Dubbel syrup from the recipe for the Dubbel Panna Cotta (see page 140). You could also soak some raisins in this syrup before adding.

MALT ICE CREAM

Two choices here and neither contain beer. The first is to add 2oz (50g) of crushed pale malt to the cream and heat for 10 minutes before straining and continuing the process as above. The second is to use only 2oz (50g) sugar and add to that 2oz (50g) of a malted

BEER STYLE: IMPERIAL STOUT

EAT IT WITH...

It can be hard to match these given how the cold ice cream dulls the tastebuds. The best option is a strong Imperial Stout served cold. If you want the best advice, then don't worry about putting a beer with the ice cream—just serve something good and strong after the bowls are emptied.

drink mix (such as Horlicks®), then at the point when you'd normally add beer, add 2 tablespoons of malt extract. You could also add some milk chocolate at the end of the process when there's still enough heat to melt it. Crumble some Maltesers® over the finished ice cream when you serve.

VIETNAMESE COFFEE STOUT ICE CREAM

This uses a different approach and makes ice cream using condensed milk—it's great as it's sweet, smooth, and doesn't require churning. This recipe is inspired by Vietnamese coffee, which is super-strong, viscous, and intense, and sweetened by a spoonful of condensed milk. Combine 1 can (around 14fl oz/400ml) of condensed milk with 2½ cups (600ml) heavy (double) cream. Add 6–8 shots of espresso (make sure this is cold) and ⅓ cup (100ml) of Imperial Stout, then freeze. Those basic measurements of ⅔ cup (400ml) of condensed milk, 2½ cups (600ml) of heavy (double), cream, and ⅓ cup (100ml) of beer can be adapted to many different recipes and beers.

EAT IT WITH...

A Doppelbock or German Weizenbock (which also works
well in the recipe). Good choices for both include Ayinger
Celebrator Doppelbock, Schneider Aventinus, or Avery
The Kaiser Imperial Oktoberfest.

OKTOBERFEST CHEESECAKE

This cheesecake is inspired by Oktoberfest. It takes many of the things that you'll see at the world's greatest drinking event and combines them into one *sehr gut* dessert. Ginger cookies (biscuits) help form the base (you'll see decorated versions hanging from stalls); there are pretzels because it's Oktoberfest and so, of course, there are pretzels; it has a layer of salted caramel apples, inspired by candied apples on sticks; and there's beer, obviously, with the best choice being a rich Doppelbock which has plenty of sweetness and low bitterness.

SERVES 8

FOR THE CHEESECAKE BASE

4½oz (125g) ginger cookies (biscuits)
3oz (75g) salted pretzels (the kind
   that you snack on in bars)
6 tablespoons (75g) butter

FOR THE SALTED CARAMEL APPLES

4 tablespoons (50g) butter
2 tablespoons brown sugar
2 eating apples, peeled, cored,
   and diced
2 tablespoons Bock or Doppelbock
Pinch of cinnamon
½ teaspoon salt

FOR THE BEER CREAM

¾ cup (200ml) heavy (double) cream
4 tablespoons Bock or Doppelbock
2 tablespoons confectioners' (icing)
   sugar
1 teaspoon vanilla extract
14oz (400g) mascarpone cheese

1 To make the cheesecake base, crush the cookies (biscuits) and pretzels to a fine mix and place in a mixing bowl. (You can also blitz the cookies and pretzels in a blender.)

2 Melt the butter in a saucepan and then mix in with the crushed cookies (biscuits) and pretzels.

3 Transfer the mixture to a large (8in/20cm) spring-form tin. Firm down the mixture, pushing it into the edges of the tin. (You can also use smaller, individual tins, if you wish.) Chill the cheesecake base in the refrigerator.

4 To make the salted caramel apples, melt the butter in a saucepan, add the sugar, and cook for a few minutes until the sugar caramelizes.

5 Mix in the apples and beer and cook for 2–3 minutes, stirring regularly.

6 Mix in the cinnamon and salt, and then set the pan to one side and allow to cool.

7 To make the beer cream, whip together the heavy (double) cream, beer, confectioners' (icing) sugar, and vanilla extract until thick. Stir in the mascarpone cheese.

8 Layer the beer cream on top of the cheesecake base and place in the refrigerator.

9 When the apples are cooled, spread them over the top of the beer cream and leave the finished cheesecake in the refrigerator for a couple of hours or until you're ready to eat.

SAISON LEMON MERINGUE PIES

SERVES 6-8

FOR THE SAISON LEMON CURD
MAKES 2-3 X 14OZ (400G) JARS

Zest and juice of 4 lemons
1 cup (200g) superfine (caster) sugar
7 tablespoons (100g) butter
Pinch of salt
3 eggs, plus 1 beaten egg yolk
4 tablespoons Saison

FOR THE PIE BASE

6 tablespoons (75g) butter
5½oz (150g) malted milk biscuits
   or Graham crackers (digestive
   biscuits), crushed

FOR THE SAISON SWISS MERINGUE

3 egg whites
½ cup (100g) superfine (caster) sugar
2 tablespoons Saison

FOR THE ICE CREAM

You can use store-bought vanilla or make your own. Follow the recipe for the Best Beer Ice Creams on page 130. Use the condensed-milk method and add the zest of one lemon.

This recipe is inspired by Lemon Icebox Pie. My version uses malt biscuits as a base, tops it with ice cream, beer lemon curd, and then a beer Swiss meringue that is blow-torched when you serve. Together you get sweetness, acidity, and the marshmallow softness of the meringue. The lemon curd lasts in the refrigerator for weeks—it's excellent on toast.

1 To make the lemon curd, combine the lemon zest, lemon juice, sugar, butter, and salt in a heatproof bowl and place over a saucepan of simmering water. When melted and thick, add the eggs and stir constantly for 10 minutes. Remove from the heat and add the beer. Transfer to sterilized jars (see page 4), allow to cool, and then store in a cool place.

2 To make the pie base, melt the butter in a saucepan and mix in the crushed biscuits. Press the mixture into individual loose-bottomed molds and chill in the refrigerator for at least 1 hour.

3 To make the meringue, whisk together the egg whites and sugar in a heatproof bowl, then place the bowl over a saucepan of simmering water, whisking until the sugar dissolves—3–5 minutes is fine. (Use an electric hand-whisk to do this.)

4 Remove the meringue mix from the heat and continue to whisk until you get thick, stiff peaks—5–10 minutes is about right. When the mixture is almost at the right consistency, add the beer a little at a time, then continue to whisk until you've used all of the beer. Allow to cool. When serving, it's easiest to put the meringue in a piping bag.

5 To make the pies, spread a tablespoon or two of Saison Lemon Curd over the biscuit bases. Top with a scoop of ice cream and then pipe on the meringue. Brown the meringue by placing under a very hot broiler (grill) for a very short amount of time or use a kitchen blowtorch (if you have one this is far more fun).

EAT IT WITH...

This is a tough beer match to nail given the sweetness and the sharp lemon curd. The best choice is a strong Belgian beer, ideally one that's been barrel-aged, where you get sticky sweetness and vanilla oak, plus a zesty spiciness from the yeast. Look for Allagash Curieux for Bourbon-infused Tripel, the Belgian-brewed Cornet Oaked Blonde, with it's vanilla edges, or try a Liefman's Kriek Brut for its sweet-sour cherry loveliness.

MAKES 1 CAKE

1½ sticks (175g) butter (at room temperature)
1⅔ cup (200g) self-raising flour
Scant 1 cup (175g) superfine (caster) sugar
3 eggs
Zest and juice 1 lemon
¼ cup (50ml) Framboise (or any raspberry beer)
7oz (200g) raspberries

FOR THE CAKE GLAZE

¼ cup (50g) superfine (caster) sugar
Juice of 2 lemons
⅓ cup (100ml) Framboise (or any raspberry beer)

FRAMBOISE LEMON CAKE

Lemon cake is delicious and this made me think: how could I possibly make it even more delicious? It wasn't a big step to go from sour fruit to sour fruit beer. The beer gives fruitiness and acidity, working so well with the lemon juice, while the raspberries cook into the cake and turn soft and sweet. It's also the kind of cake that will last for a few days and stay tasty and moist—if you'll allow it to.

1 Preheat the oven to 325°F/160°C/Gas 3. Butter a deep loose-bottomed cake tin (around 8in/20cm in diameter).

2 Use an electric mixer to cream together the butter, flour, sugar, and eggs in a mixing bowl until thick and smooth.

3 Mix in the remaining ingredients then gently stir in the raspberries before pouring the batter into the cake tin. Bake for around 50–60 minutes (using a skewer to check that the cake is cooked through—it may need less or more time depending on how deep your cake tin is). Place on a wire rack.

4 While the cake is still warm, make the glaze by mixing together all the ingredients. Take a skewer and pierce small holes through the cake, then brush over the glaze. Allow to cool before serving.

BEER STYLE:
COFFEE STOUT

EAT IT WITH...

The raspberry beer you use in this naturally works really well, though it can be a bit too much sour-on-sour with the sugar just muddling it up. The lateral-thinking option is to go for coffee and the roasted bitterness and subtle acidity of a Coffee Stout. To Øl Goliat Imperial Coffee Stout, Dieu du Ciel Péché Mortel, or Siren's Broken Dream are the top choices.

7oz (200g) semi-sweet (dark) chocolate, minimum 70% cocoa solids
Pinch of salt
2 tablespoons superfine (caster) sugar
Zest and juice of 1 large orange
4 eggs, separated
$\frac{1}{3}$ cup (100ml) Double IPA

CHOCOLATE ORANGE DOUBLE IPA MOUSSE

This mousse is easy to make and a great way to get the big citrus aroma of the beer into a dessert, where any hop bitterness is sweetened by the chocolate–for the best-tasting versions use the most aromatic Double IPA you can find; ideally, one with sweetness and relatively low bitterness. It's light, yet feels decadent, and it works well with the beer used in it, so you can carry on drinking Double IPA with dessert.

1 Melt the chocolate in a heatproof bowl over a saucepan of simmering water.

2 Stir in the salt, half of the sugar, the orange zest (reserving some for decoration), and 4 tablespoons of fresh orange juice. Remove from the heat.

3 Add the egg yolks, mixing them into the hot chocolate mixture, followed by the beer.

4 In a separate bowl, whisk the egg whites until they form stiff peaks. Halfway through whisking the egg whites, add the remaining sugar. When firm, gently fold the egg white mixture into the chocolate.

5 Pour the mousse into separate serving bowls, sprinkle the reserved orange zest on top, and place in the refrigerator for a few hours (or overnight).

EAT IT WITH...

Double IPA works well here as it can handle the sweetness and mirrors the flavor in the recipe. Just make sure it has malt sweetness and, ideally, the bitterness won't be too high—it'll all be aroma. Try Avery Brewing's Maharajah, Buxton Nth Cloud, or Epic Brewing's Hop Zombie.

DUBBEL PANNA COTTA

This is one of the easiest desserts there is, but it's also one of the most impressive and pleasing to eat. Unlike a crème brûlée, which requires a custard base, this is simply cream set with gelatine and that's a wonderful canvas to take on other flavors. My favorite version uses Dubbel, which has a toasty, spicy, dried-fruit depth. I've made an excellent version, which simply adds 4 tablespoons of beer to the cream mix, but I like the more intense flavor that comes from reducing the beer– it's a rare example of when doing this works.

SERVES 4-6

6 sheets of gelatine (approx. ¼oz/8g)
2½ cups (600ml) heavy (double) cream
½ cup (100g) superfine (caster) sugar
1 cinnamon stick
¾ cup (200ml) whole milk
⅔ cup (150ml) Dubbel
1 tablespoon dark brown sugar

TO SERVE (OPTIONAL):

4–6 plums or peaches (stoned) or apples (peeled and cored)
Around ⅔ cup (150ml) Dubbel
2 tablespoons brown sugar
Juice of 1 orange
1 cinnamon stick

1 Soak the gelatine leaves in a large bowl of cold water for 10 minutes.

2 Meanwhile, combine the cream and sugar in a large saucepan, add the cinnamon stick, and warm gently for 1 minute. Remove from the heat and take out the cinnamon stick.

3 Take the gelatine sheets and squeeze out the excess water. Whisk the gelatine into the cream. Pour in the milk, then strain through a sieve into a large pouring jug.

4 Stir the beer and brown sugar together in a saucepan over a medium heat and allow the liquid to bubble and reduce to half its volume–this should only take a minute.

5 Pour the beer and sugar mixture into a bowl, allow to cool for 10 minutes, and then mix into the cream.

6 Pour the mixture into individual ramekins. Leave to cool, then place in the refrigerator for 4–12 hours before serving.

TO SERVE: This is good enough to serve alone, but you might like to bake some plums or apples in a small baking dish with the remaining beer from the bottle, some sugar, orange juice, and a cinnamon stick at 400°F/200°C/Gas 6 for around 15 minutes to serve on the side.

BEER STYLE: QUADRUPEL

EAT IT WITH...
Step up from Dubbel to Quad and pour something like St Bernardus Abt 12, Straffe Hendrik Quadrupel, or Dieu du Ciel Rigor Mortis. The beers all have chewy dried fruits, brown sugar, toasted nuts, and seasonal spice, plus lively carbonation to keep it refreshing.

INDEX

ACKNOWLEDGMENTS

Cooking is fun because you get to eat at the end of it. Eating is best when you share that food with other people. Add in some beers—the most social drink in the world—and it's even better. The best part about writing this book was sharing the food and beer with others.

The usual thanks go to my always hungry and thirsty mates who never turn down food or beer, and who also helped cook some recipes and gave me ideas or feedback on what I'd made. Cheers Matt Stokes, Mark Charlwood, Pete Brissenden, and Chris Perrin.

My kitchen was busy and messy for months and I thank Will Lake for putting up with that. Somehow you managed to miss most of the actual food, so I guess I owe you dinner.

Cheers to Martyn Cornell for guidance in the history of cooking with beer.

Thanks to Pete Jorgensen and Cindy Richards—you let me write books and that's still a dream for me. Thanks to Caroline West for editing, Eoghan O'Brien for the design, and to Alex Luck, Laura Urschel, Luis Peral, and Kerry Lewis for all their work organizing, preparing, styling, and shooting the food. Seeing the recipes I'd cooked at home turn into the photographs in this book is an amazing thing.

My love of cooking comes from my mum. She cooked every day when I was growing up: there were always cakes during the week, wonderful stews, pies, desserts, and roast dinners on Sundays. And my family always sat down to dinner together. That was an important part of growing up and mealtimes were at the heart of it. Homemade Christmas pudding using strong ale was my first—and still one of my favorite—recipes using beer.

Emma, you ate most of the things that I cooked and even toward the end of this you were still eager to try more. You make everything more fun and wonderful and exciting.